S0-AER-187

EASY GREEN

EASY GREEN

A HANDBOOK OF EARTH-SMART ACTIVITIES AND OPERATING PROCEDURES FOR YOUTH PROGRAMS

MARTY WESTERMAN

American Camping Association ®

Copyright 1993 American Camping Association, Inc.

Printed in the United States of America

All rights reserved. No part of this book may be reproduced or transmitted in any form or by any means, electronic or mechanical, including photocopying, recording, or any information storage and retrieval system, without permission in writing from the publisher.

The forms in this book were intended to be helpful in building your environmental program. You may photocopy any of the forms in this book for use in your program, presentations to your board of directors, or other operational uses. For additional uses, please write to the publisher.

American Camping Association
5000 State Road 67 North
Martinsville, IN 46151-7902

317/342-8456 American Camping Association National Office
800/428-CAMP American Camping Association Bookstore
317/342-2065 FAX

The publisher wishes to thank Seattle (WA) Tilth Association for its permission to render the bin designs and specifications in Chapter 9 and Appendix C.

Library of Congress Cataloging-in-Publication Data

Westerman, Marty.
    Easy green :   a handbook of earth-smart operating
  procedures and activities for youth programs / Marty Westerman.
        p.   cm.
    Includes bibliographical references.
    ISBN 0-87603-132-7
    1. Environmental protection—Study and teaching.   2. Environmental
    education—Activity programs.   3. Campfire programs.   I. Title.
TD170.6.W47   1993
628—dc20

92-47349
CIP

CONTENTS

CHAPTER 6
ENERGY CONSERVATION

CHAPTER 7
PRECYCLING SUPPLIES AND SUPPLIERS

CHAPTER 8
RECYCLING

INTRODUCTION

"It is not incumbent on you to finish the task, but neither are you free to desist from it."
—Rabbi Judah c.200, Mishna Perke Avot 2:16 (Ethics of the Fathers)

America's camps are small towns where active citizens live, eat, and play, just as they do at home. Unfortunately, they also throw out tons of food and other waste products, and they use as much water and energy as small towns do. Escalating costs for these resources, and a growing body of local, state, and federal laws on hazardous materials, liability, and waste management mean no one should run a day or resident camp today without being environmentally aware.

Perhaps more importantly, we are in a unique position to impact the future. Many of our campers and staff members study society's new "three Rs" year-round: reduce, reuse, and recycle. Camps are great places to reinforce this lesson because operators and participants live the experience as a team.

It was this sense of teamwork that prompted me to write this book. During the late 1980s, campers and staff members at California's Brandeis-Bardin Institute's (BBI) two camps, Alonim and Brandeis Collegiate Institute, questioned the environmental wisdom behind a number of supply, operational, and programming practices. In early 1990, BBI director Alvin Mars, program director Arthur Pinchev, and finance officer Howard Kaplan decided to make key environmental policy changes, and invited me to help create and run their new environmental program. At the time, I was an environmental journalist, having published articles in several environmental trade and popular magazines, and I served as a recycling consultant for the National Softdrink Association.

That season, BBI bought permanent dishware and stopped using disposable utensils except for picnics and the occasional weekend meal. The two camp kitchens, which served 1,500 meals a day, collected 1,000 pounds of cardboard, metal, paper, and glass *every week* for recycling and put out nearly 4,000 pounds of food waste to compost.

Over the season, the two camps cut their trash output in half, saving approximately $3,000 in hauling fees, and recycled a quantity of paper and cardboard equivalent to two dozen pulpable trees. The metal they recycled saved enough energy to light three American homes for a year (at 131 kwh use per month).

The camps also purchased low-flow heads for the showers and put displacers in all tank toilets. This cut water demand by nearly 300,000 gallons.

I won't pretend we accomplished all this without a hitch. We had many disagreements and difficulties, primarily because we didn't realize how much time and effort it would take to implement a comprehensive environmental program on this scale. So rather than encourage you to dive into a total program, I caution you to heed the lessons we learned:

❏ Proceed one step at a time.

❏ Integrate each step into camp programs.

❏ Get the support of the camp board, staff, and campers for each step.

The fruits of my subsequent environmental research and professional experiences are detailed in this book. Its goals are to

❏ Help camp directors and programmers make informed environmental choices, and

❏ Help them make environmental awareness a habit in all operations, programming, and activities.

This book covers everything from A to Z: Aerator shower heads to your climate Zone. There are worksheets to help you organize and plan specific strategies for hazardous materials, toxics reduction, energy and water conservation, supply reduction, recycling, and composting. The book also includes programming ideas, resources, and brief summaries of environmental issues that should prove helpful in determining how "the big picture" will affect your operation over time.

In addition to the benefits to your bottom line, your environmental efforts may well start your participants on new endeavors. BBI's 1990 alumni have not only introduced their parents to recycling, but have written school reports on environmental issues, given public speeches on this topic, published newsletter articles, and started environmental programs at their schools, community centers, places of employment and worship.

I dedicate this handbook to those people who participated in BBI's inaugural program and to those who have continued the camps' ecology programs. I also dedicate it to all camping personnel who want to create environment-friendly operations and programs.

Marty Westerman
Seattle, 1993

ACKNOWLEDGEMENTS

Every book is a team effort, and I want to thank those who helped and supported me through this labor. First, my wife, Eddie, for introducing me to Brandeis-Bardin Institute, and for her continued support, encouragement, and programming contributions. Next, programming whiz Marla Cohen, now at Hillel Santa Cruz, for her detailed proofreading and camp program input in Chapters 2 and 3; my American Camping Association in-house editor and her team; Chaz Miller for reviews and encouragement; friends, experts, and idea people Dan Kennedy, Bill Kunin, Rabbi Bob Davis, and Harry Brechner; and specialists Mark Hauser, Mitch Mamegawa, Carl Woest-Wind, Ray Hoffman, Jim Jensen, Craig Benton, Howard Stenn, George at Jorgensen, Julie Nakao, Michelle Hadley, Dave Wirth, Dave Kolan, Dave Brown, and Darwin Nordin.

1
BEGINNINGS

1
PHILOSOPHY AND OPTIONS

"This is the first time we've ever done this, so we're doing better than we ever did before."
—Arthur Pinchev, BBI program director

Ecologically speaking, any camp in the country faces four challenges:

❏ Creating an environmental philosophy that fosters ecologically sensible programs,

❏ Demonstrating how actions affect the environment,

❏ Teaching alternative behaviors to protect the earth, so that participants can think and act independently in this area, and

❏ Becoming environmentally profitable as well as environmentally friendly.

Ultimately, you want all participants in your camp's program to act from a sense of empathy with the earth.

PHILOSOPHICAL BUILDING BLOCKS

Our ancient ancestors, whether they lived in Africa, the Americas, Australia, or Europe, shared certain beliefs:

❏ The individual, tribe, and earth mutually depended on each other for their health, and

❏ Individuals were responsible for supporting the well-being of the tribe or community, and the earth (what we now call "ecosystem") where they lived.

The specific philosophies of individual religions and races varied, however, just as your camp's environmental policy will differ from another's in the next state.

Nearly 3,000 years ago, early Buddhists introduced the idea that humans and their environment were the same. Any sickness in one created, or was reflected as, a sickness in the other. For humans to heal their environment, they had to heal themselves. This involved being aware of the moment, living simply, and in many cases prizing life and principles above money and technology. Their philosophy has remained virtually the same throughout the centuries and has spawned Taoism, Confucianism, Hinduism, and Shintoism.

In Australia, the Aboriginals believed their ancestors—the lizard, ostrich, emu, koala, and other great animals—formed themselves from the earth, and sang the world into being as a perfect place. Along each "song line" on this great island, each ancestor placed water, game, vegetation, and shelter for its human tribe to use. Tampering with these song lines, beyond getting food and shelter, endangered all life that depended on them.

Many American Indian nations declared there is life in everything: animals, trees, rocks, the sky. Whenever they took some of that life it had to be for a purpose, such as feeding and sheltering the tribe, and they had to include thanks to the Great Spirit who created it. They took only as much as they needed, and they acknowledged that their actions would affect the world for seven generations to come. Both nomadic and stable tribes traveled recognized territories, but neither practiced land ownership. They believed the Great Spirit owned the earth and provided it for humans to use. Because no person owned land, everyone had to take responsibility for it since others always would use the earth after them.

In the Middle East, ancient nomadic Israelites established several concepts with positive environmental impacts: A day of rest each week for humans and animals, and a year of rest in every seven for farmland. They believed—and still do—that the community is responsible for an individual's actions, and the individual is responsible for community actions.

The main Jewish tenet against waste is found in their rules of war, written in the Torah (also known as the Old Testament). In Deuteronomy 20:19, siege armies are warned not to harm the fruit trees surrounding an enemy city: "Are (trees) men, that you should make war against them?" Later Jewish scholars have extended this passage to forbid wasting food, fuel, land, or materials; to breaking objects in anger; and to causing pain to humans and animals.

An environmental ethic in Christianity has only emerged in the past few decades, combining elements from the Jewish, Asian, and American Indian ideals, and from the passionate, creation-centered spirituality of Meister Eckhart, a 14th-Century priest whose works were suppressed for centuries by the Catholic Church. Matthew Fox, in his *Breakthrough—Meister Eckhart's Creational Spirituality in New Translation,* asserts that creation-centered spirituality is Jewish, biblical, and prophetic, and that it includes respect for the earth and all its peoples, animals, and plants, and love of arts, the human form, passion, and politics. Fox laments that in the centuries since Eckhart, the West has almost lost this spiritual tradition.

A century before Christianity, two Hebrew sages, Hillel and Shammai, debated whether or not it was good for man to have been created at all (Talmud, Erubin 13b). Hillel argued it was; Shammai disagreed. The wise men eventually decided man should not be here, but since humans had been created, they should make the best of it, by "searching their deeds"—that is, developing a strong sense of conscience.

Along that line today, a group spearheaded by prominent scientists and Jewish and Christian leaders, formed in 1991 to further interfaith environmental efforts. Based in New York City, the Joint Appeal In Religion And Science (see Appendix A) publishes *A Guide to Environmental Activities in the American Religious Community*, which provides a summary of current Jewish and Christian environmental statements and activities across the nation. Editor Cheryl Cook says it represents "a relatively new undertaking for the religious communities: a sense of activism on behalf of the natural environment."

National youth and camping groups have taken steps toward addressing environmental issues, too.

Both the Boy Scouts of America and Girl Scouts of the U.S.A. encourage their members to create programs and lead lives that have little to no negative impact on the environment. They encourage activities that minimize pollution, conserve water and energy resources, and reduce waste. The Law of Girl Scouting includes the pledge to "use resources wisely, and protect and improve the world around me." The *Boy Scout Handbook* says: "Accept responsibility for the Earth as a sign of getting maturity and wisdom."

The largest youth organization in the world, the U.S. Department of Agriculture-sponsored 4-H (Head, Heart, Hand, Health), has launched a new experiential education program it calls Environmental Stewardship. Its goal is to teach "a commitment to responsible resource management which contributes to the quality of life for present and future generations. This includes knowing about and caring for the environment, and applying this concern through responsible action for the rest of our lives."

The American Camping Association's (ACA) *Exemplary Ethical Practices for Camp Directors/Owners* asks directors and owners to develop an ecological conscience and recognize that "a thing is right when it tends to preserve the integrity, stability, and beauty of the biotic community."

CREATING A PHILOSOPHY

What you do in your environment is important, but the reason for doing it is perhaps more vital than your actions themselves.

"Value" is the best place to begin developing an environmental philosophy. But how do you instill value in things that, until recently, Western civilization valued only for their immediate worth, if it valued them at all?

In a capitalist society, commercial enterprises tend to evaluate resources only for their contributions to products and services. A housing developer values a piece of land on a lake, a paper company values the pine trees it uses for pulp, an electric utility values water or coal used to generate energy, and an insurance company values electricity to power its lights, telephones, and computers.

This assessment system is too narrow because each singly valued resource is part of an ecosystem, which in turn is part of a biome. How we use each resource affects the health of related insects, animals, plants, land, and sometimes, the climate. Ecologist Aldo Leopold defines health as a biotic system's "capacity for self-renewal" in *A Sand County Almanac*.

There are 20 major North American ecosystems, which are inter-related communities of plants and animals. Examples include the Alaskan tundra, the Florida Everglades, Hawaiian rainforests, and the Southwestern hot deserts. (See Figure 1-1.)

What Is a Biome?

A biome is a regional group of related ecosystems, identified by climate, topography, and soil. The North American continent supports six biomes, from arctic and arctic tundra near the North Pole to coniferous forests, temperate deciduous forests, grasslands, and, finally, deserts near the Mexican border.

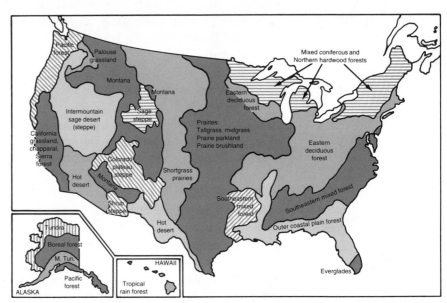

Figure 1-1. North American Ecoregions (Source: Adapted from R.G. Bailey, 1976. Ecoregions of the United States. *U.S. Department of Agriculture's Forest Service in cooperation with the U.S. Fish and Wildlife Service.)*

There are still other resources society barely values at all. Air, protective atmosphere, biodiversity, and a healthy planet are still considered "externalities" in the commercial sector; that is, items that aren't directly related to creating products and services. Society currently uses these resources for "free" (at least there's no financial charge), so they are generally taken for granted. Because the commercial world is not eager to begin paying for these resources, it's happy to support the belief that they are inexhaustible and perpetually self-renewing and so they have less value than short-term development interests.

However, research over the past several decades has shown otherwise: This planet's resources and self-renewal processes are finite. As a result, economists, accountants, lawyers, and private citizens are discovering that one way to protect natural resources in a capitalist society is simply to assign them more monetary value. Which, of course, brings us back to the original question: How do you practically accomplish this task?

Start by emulating the method California used to revalue its air: Levy a penalty on those who abuse the resource. In the late 1970s, California enacted laws that require automobiles to pass both the federal emission control standards and the state's emission control standards biannually in order to be registered. According to the state's Bureau of Motor Vehicles, if the driver of an out-of-state vehicle is pulled over for any moving violation, has been in the state 20 days or longer, and cannot prove compliance with California emission control law, he or she can be fined $300.

Another strategy is to offer a reward for those who comply with your values. For example, many states are revaluing air, space, and gasoline resources by providing a fast lane, or high-occupancy vehicle lanes for carpoolers. Solo drivers must remain in the heavy-traffic, slower lanes.

There's a case to be made for old-fashioned complaining, too. The firm, and sometimes dramatic, demands of non-smokers for clean air spaces over the last 20 years have prompted action by restaurant owners, airport designers, and other public facility operators. Today non-smoking sections are the rule nearly everywhere. Some public places enforce non-smoking rules throughout their entire establishments.

Few creatures on this planet can survive without air. If you cannot quantify the value of human life, the value of the air on which it depends is priceless. The same is true for other survival resources: water, earth, diverse flora and fauna, and the ozone layer that protects us from being toasted by ultraviolet rays. Each of these resources has aesthetic values you need to consider in your camp's overall philosophy as well.

Creating a camp environmental philosophy begins with assigning definite values to your camp's resources and surrounding area. Ideally, you, your staff, and campers will learn a new ABC: Always Be Conscious.

To begin the valuation exercises for your environmental philosophy, ask yourself the following questions:

❏ How does the quality of your air affect campers and staff at your camp? Do flowers, grasses, trees, water, or activity spaces give off characteristic scents that identify the "smell" of camp? Do these smells trigger pleasant reactions from your staff and guests? What value do you place on this?

❏ Can you see the stars in the night sky? If housing developments begin encroaching on your borders, their lights can fade the inky black sky to gray, making the stars more difficult to see. How does this affect your sense of the camp's value?

❏ If your camp has a lake, do the staff and campers believe it's important to swim and boat there? Would they be content to only view it if it was polluted? Or would they go elsewhere to camp at a clean lake? Likewise, as an operator or director, how does this lake benefit your operation in terms of aesthetics (property enhancement) and attracting campers (tangible income)?

SAMPLE CAMP ENVIRONMENT PHILOSOPHY

Using others' philosophical approaches and your own camp's valuations, write a formal environmental statement. Yours could look similar to this:

We are an integral part of the _____ ecosystem. We value the earth, clean air, clean water, healthy people, plants, animals, and insects—both indoors and outdoors. We will live in balance with our ecosystem, and minimize our negative impact on this environment. We will take care of our resources—from our air to our water, to our food, and to the creatures who share this planet with us—so we may enjoy them tomorrow and pass their beauty to future generations.

When translating these words into action, you may consider adopting the guidelines of Holden Village, a Lutheran conference center on Lake Chelan near the Cascade Mountains in Washington:

❑ All purchase orders indicate that goods shipped in non-recyclable packing material will be returned.

❑ Non-recyclable packing material that cannot be returned is reused, but a note is sent to the packer discouraging production of this material. Rather than buying more, we are reusing this.

❑ Informational materials sent to incoming staff and guests indicate that non-recyclable material should not be brought into camp.

❑ A no-charge diaper service to discourage use of disposables is available.

❑ An active advocacy program of letter writing educates and encourages environmentally sensitive production and the use of durable and recyclable products.

❑ All staff serve on teams that sort waste for recycling and disposal. All guests are encouraged to join these teams as part of the educational program. Also, the center is committed to dealing with its own disposable waste rather than shipping it to another waste disposal site.

❑ The staff repairs damaged items rather than purchase replacements.

❑ The staff purchases quality goods that will last and can be repaired.

❑ The staff purchases used products before new.

❑ The staff purchases recyclable products and products produced with recycled material.

PHILOSOPHY INTO ACTION

Now it's time to tackle the next steps in developing a sound environmental policy: Demonstrating how our actions affect the environment and teaching alternative behaviors to protect it. (You can find specific programming ideas in Chapters 2 and 3).

Approximately 60 percent of North American camps offer some form of environmental education, according to ACA's *Guide to Accredited Camps*. Some are dedicated environmental camps, although most offer environmental activities and education as "something else" to do. What you decide to offer at your camp hinges on many factors: the type of camp you have and your facilities, programs, available budget, staff, and local resources. The challenge is making the environment an immediate concern, and one that participants are conscious of, whether the program emphasis is on sports, the arts, religion, the outdoors, or another area.

Although camps may be in session for only a few weeks and are often physically isolated, they function as small towns. And each camp still depends on civilization for its survival—and continues to consume and discard products in the process every day. So don't assume your camp can avoid making an environmental impact. Its space alone has already been carved out of the wilderness, a city park, or a community center yard, which interrupted the ecosystem. But don't despair; you still can minimize the camp's impact without inconveniencing staff and guests. The secret lies in moving toward minimum impact one step at a time.

WHERE TO BEGIN

"The environment" covers a lot of ground. Before you can hope to be successful in your new mission, you must break the subject into manageable chunks to discover the options that give you the best "leverage" for your investment of people, time, and money. In the language of economics, this concept is called "opportunity cost." Then use the worksheets in succeeding chapters to create manageable plans.

Here are some options you may wish to consider, although you may need to analyze answers to many other questions as well:

❏ Is it a better use of your camp's resources to collect all materials for recycling—steel, aluminum, plastics, glass, mixed paper, and cardboard—whether or not they can be recycled locally? Or will you collect only those materials that can be locally recycled? The first action requires storage space for the items you can't ship out now, but it sets a good example for participants. The latter action demonstrates how to live within the practical limits of reality.

❏ If you plan to develop your facility as a year-round conference center, you will use your buildings in every season. That may require renovations and upgrades. Where will you get the best financial and environmental return on your investment: insulating certain spaces and windows? "daylighting" buildings? changing energy sources and heating and cooling systems? landscaping with drought-tolerant plants? Your answers depend on your intentions, climate, costs for water and energy, and costs and availability of local materials and labor.

A Closer Look

*As with any staff addi-
tions, hiring an environ-
mental program director
from outside your camp
"family" instead of run-
ning it yourself or bringing up a staffer through
the ranks has its pros
and cons. Advantages:
The program director
can bring fresh ideas,
different perspectives,
and a new energy to
camp. Disadvantages:
The newcomer may not
know the camp's tradi-
tions, its procedures, or
its "family," and may
encounter resistance at
one or many levels.*

❑ Is it feasible to hire an eco-programs director to create activities that participants will carry home to do in their communities? Or should you spend the money on equipment that cuts energy and water demand for the facility? Can you do both?

❑ Can you put the money to better use if you save or invest it this year while you study your options for next? Can you afford to hire a consultant to provide you with an environmental audit and set up a multi-year step-by-step plan to follow?

OTHER CONSIDERATIONS

All camps operate in conjunction with their locality and its available supplies, people, and services. This may impose limits on your plans. But whichever environmental programs you choose to implement, plan on the following:

❑ Encourage everyone to be co-owners of the changes. It's not a matter of simply explaining policy to your board, staff, and campers. You need their support to succeed, so develop a sense of program ownership for all participants.

For example, as the director of BBI's environmental policy, I tried to explain the new recycling and composting program to the camp's head chef during Orientation Week. Nonplussed, he shrugged. "Well," he told me flatly, "I guess everybody needs a job." It was my first inkling things might not go as smoothly that summer as I had anticipated. My lesson: Get directors, the head staff, crew, anyone who will be touched by a new program together in the same place at the same time, and discuss your plans before taking that first step.

If you encounter resistance during the actual program, you may have to review how you've designed or presented the project. Usually, if you start with simpler, less involved projects, your chances for success are greater.

❑ Redesign the camp's programs and schedules. Build in the extra 10 to 20 minutes it may take your campers and staff to complete conservation-, recycling- and composting-related tasks. Understand also that sometimes participants in your environmental activities may be late to their next activity. In some cases, you may even have to reschedule activities that follow environmental tasks.

SUPPLIERS' STRENGTHS AND LIMITATIONS By now, most suppliers are aware of new water and energy conservation equipment, optional building materials, packaging, and recyclable and recycled consumer products. But not all suppliers stock or sell such items. And because manufacturing and supply networks are still being developed, prices for these goods are sometimes higher than those for standard equipment. As the supply and demand for alternative products equals that of virgin material products, prices will be more competitive.

If suppliers or tradespeople try to dissuade you from using the newer alternatives, make sure they can back their objections with facts. These arguments may be framed as suggestions: "Stick with what you have—that's the way it comes from the manufacturer," "Everybody uses that product successfully the way it is," or "This permanent item is much more expensive, and won't last long enough to justify the increased cost over disposables." Counter by asking for details on an actual customer who was satisfied (or dissatisfied) with the newer product.

You may have to research the alternative product on your own if your supplier can't offer customer satisfaction statistics and other background information. Then, once you get the new product, test to see if it works better than the old one, and keep your supplier informed. If you approach this as a partnership with your salesperson, it can be a win-win situation for both.

Your camp's ultimate challenge is to create a world where it is in everyone's self-interest to support the environment and the people who live in it. Appendix A lists publications and catalog companies that sell alternative products.

LOCALITY STRENGTHS AND LIMITATIONS When it comes to establishing a recycling program, you are dependent on what recyclers in your locality will accept (see Chapter 8 for more information). In some areas, they may only take cardboard and aluminum. Other recyclers collect everything. To get the scoop on your area, call your municipal or county solid waste department, your contract trash hauler, and check the *Yellow Pages* listings under "Recycling."

Some camps can donate food scraps to a local farmer or rancher; if this option is possible in your locality, ask your agricultural extension agent if the practice is legal in your state (see Chapter 9 for more information, and Appendix A for further reading and resources).

Local utilities are often great resources for energy and water conservation information. Many power and water companies provide free literature, compare your past years' bills, and do free on-site surveys to help you get started. Many water companies provide "conservation kits" that include toilet-tank displacer bags, shower flow-restricter discs, and pamphlets on conserving water (see Chapter 5 for more information).

Many utilities also offer rebates and low- or zero-interest loan programs for customers who are retrofitting their facilities. And, if you devise a way to generate electric power at camp, the electric utility is obliged by law to buy your excess electricity. All these options can help offset the costs of your environmental program.

Local entities, in addition to state and federal agencies, regulate hazardous and toxic material disposal. Contact your municipal or county solid waste and ecology or environment department for details on local regulations and disposal options. For answers on federal regulations, call or write your regional Environmental Protection Agency office (see Chapter 4 and Appendix A for more information).

Most of the items and equipment mentioned in this book are readily available at any local hardware or building supply store. Whatever you can't find locally, you can order from catalogs (see listings in Appendix A). If you order by mail, factor delivery times into your schedule.

FACILITY STRENGTHS AND LIMITATIONS These depend upon several concerns:

❑ ownership (do you own or rent? Can you proceed with your plans on your own, or do you need permissions from someone else?)

❑ facility size (e.g., large, with grounds, or small, inside a building)

❑ facility location (urban, suburban, rural)

❑ age and condition of your physical plant (sewer, plumbing, electrical, structures, equipment, etc.) and

❑ your available budget and future plans

Ownership is key: who makes the decisions about your camp's plans? If you or your board do, you can follow one process. But if someone else owns your facility, you may need their agreement before proceeding. Still, whatever your camp's circumstances, most upgrades are so beneficial (i.e., cutting energy and water demands, reducing waste, improving structures) that your decision-makers should find them too good to refuse.

Facility size dictates another set of circumstances: On what scale can you make plans and how extensive can they be? How much storage space can you devote to collecting recyclable materials? Do you have space for composting activities?

Physical plant age and condition basically determine costs. The older the plant, the more expensive it can be to upgrade, and this may limit the scope of changes you can afford to make. For example, adding toilet tank displacers may not be too expensive, but lighting or appliance upgrades may require unacceptable expenses for rewiring and new circuit breakers.

To get work done, of course, you can arrange trade-outs and donations, recruit volunteers from your board, camp alumni, local residents and businesses, even partner with your utilities, community colleges, and tradespeople. The possibilities are endless. As a last resort, you can buy your supplies and pay somebody to do the labor.

STAFF STRENGTHS AND LIMITATIONS Successful companies like 3M, IBM, Frito-Lay, Chrysler, Starbuck's, and Nordstrom keep their staff members well-trained, informed, and encouraged to take responsibility, so everyone—top to bottom—has a stake in making things work.

Camps are showcases for this type of management. Staffs are hired to take responsibility from the beginning and to create enjoyable and enriching experiences for their campers. Some staff members may be ecologically conscious and consequently excited by this opportunity to help train campers in it. Their excitement is contagious; capitalize on it.

The strengths of your staff members are their enthusiasm and their knowledge of what has and has not worked for each of them in their own camping experiences. Their limitations may be in accepting and implementing new ideas and unfamiliar programs. Generally, they will resist an imposed, top-down management style, and they will embrace a style that invites them to participate, add their own ideas, and create their own programs.

Your responsibility, then, is to fashion the new programs in steps with which staff members can feel comfortable, gain competence, and feel a sense of participation. Your success also depends on training and equipping the staff members during, or before, Orientation Week and providing continuing in-service training so they are not forced to learn the new routines as they try to handle the campers in that first week.

It is crucial to understand that these programs require time and people to succeed. (For example, basic recycling and composting at meal times may take KPs an extra five minutes to complete. If you don't want those activities disrupting other programs, you must factor the extra time and personnel requirements into your schedules.)

Every week during the season, keep the staff informed about how new programs are working, and what changes you are making to improve them.

CAMPERS' STRENGTHS AND LIMITATIONS Campers attend camp to enjoy themselves. How much they participate depends on how clear and consistent your programs are, and how effectively you and your staff manage the programs.

What your camp accomplishes depends on your campers' age group. In general, younger campers are more willing, even eager, to get dirty, so they usually accept the messier environmental activities such as recycling and composting. As the children enter puberty, however, they become more conscious of their appearances and less willing to do anything they consider embarrassing. By college age, they'll usually agree to do something if they agree with its philosophy.

ANTICIPATING AND HANDLING RESISTANCE

Your board or colleagues may veto environmental awareness proposals if they appear to be costly or require program changes.

To win their support, use these approaches:

1. Document the costs and benefits of your proposals in terms of dollars and improvements. Use the worksheets and resources in the following chapters for this purpose.

   In some cases, the paybacks are quick. For example, when you manage solid waste better, you'll begin reducing trash hauling costs the first month. (You also may earn a few dollars for the recyclable items.) Other strategies take time for payback, and the financial benefit is minimal. For example, the cost of finding building entrance points for rodents and insects, and then screening or sealing these openings is equivalent to what you pay for an exterminator's services. But, long-term, you will cut the financial and environmental costs of pesticide use at your camp.

   In some cases, the benefits are more aesthetic than monetary. Create new drought-tolerant landscaping, for example, and you'll add brilliant new colors to the camp and attract more varieties of birds and insects.

2. Start your environmental program with changes that involve the camp's facilities, structures, and services. For example, changing shower heads

is relatively cheap to do, limited in scope, provides documentable paybacks, and doesn't require sacrifices from your programs, staff, or campers.

3. Stress that conservation means using and paying only for what you need. For example, campers can get just as clean in a shower that flows at 3.5 gallons per minute (gpm) as in one that flows at 7.5 gpm. They also can flush a toilet just as effectively with two or three gallons of water as with five or seven gallons. And they can waste eight ounces of water trying to drink four at a fountain, or they can drink all 12 by putting it in a carry-along bottle.

Take the same approach with energy conservation. New compact fluorescent bulbs can deliver the same brightness levels as incandescents and use up to 90 percent less power. They may cost more now ($10 compared to $2), but they save power immediately, last up to 10 times longer, and save you the labor of 10 installations.

4. Explain that your costs for water, energy, and materials will only increase over the next few years, even if alternative resources are found and developed. You may even face shortages due to demand, misuse, climatic conditions (such as a drought), or all three. To maintain your supplies and keep your costs down, you want to manage with as little of these resources as possible now.

5. Make a plan, preferably a multi-year one. As with any new project, if you create a plan and stick to it, you will have fewer opportunities to get sidetracked on expensive projects not approved by your board, owner, or your own annual budget.

Here is a sample of a multi-year plan:

Year one: Reduce high-liability toxics use.

❑ Eliminate or find substitutes for toxic substances.

❑ Replace CFC-based air-conditioners, refrigerators, and freezers.

❑ Fill or remove underground tank(s).

Years one and two: Introduce materials-management efforts.

❑ Review procurement practices and audit camp inventory to reduce the quantities of products and packaging you purchase.

❑ Plan to purchase quality products that can be reused.

❑ Contact local recyclers and trash haulers to begin recycling program.

❑ Contact county cooperative extension agent or other expert to begin small-scale landscape composting program.

Years one through three: Introduce water-conservation efforts.

❑ Install low-flow, button shut-off shower heads.

❑ Install toilet-tank displacers or dams, or low-gallonage toilets.

❑ Install 5–gallon buckets in every shower and bathtub.

❑ Install rain barrels to collect water for irrigation, tool cleaning, etc. (Cover rain barrels on dry days to minimize evaporation and mosquito population growth.)

❑ Install drip irrigation lines for shrub beds, orchards, and gardens.

❏ Install water-miser dishwasher(s).

❏ Xeriscape: landscape with drought-tolerant plants.

❏ Encourage new water-saving habits such as having campers carry water bottles, turn off water while brushing their teeth and soaping in the shower, and watering landscapes before mid-morning or after sunset.

❏ Use only one tub of water when rinsing food off recyclable containers.

❏ Let the grass turn brown instead of watering the lawn.

Years one through four: Introduce energy-conservation efforts.

❏ Install low-wattage, compact fluorescent lights in all buildings.

❏ Install low-wattage street lamps, if appropriate.

❏ Install office equipment, including computers, printers, copiers and FAX machines, with "standby" or between-task automatic shut-off features.

❏ Install energy-efficient, "super-insulated" water heater(s), or on-demand water heaters, refrigerators, and freezers.

❏ Turn down water heater temperatures.

❏ Change energy sources to lowest-cost options: natural gas, propane, etc.

❏ Put all machinery and vehicles on preventive maintenance schedules.

❏ Turn off office equipment when its not in use.

❏ Turn off lights when they're not in use.

❏ Shut off vehicles if you intend to leave them running more than one minute.

FINAL THOUGHTS

Your desire to establish an environmental program at your camp is commendable. But simply wanting to do something isn't enough in this case. You first need to assign a tangible value to your natural resources, then write a formal environmental philosophy, or direction, to guide your efforts.

Next, determine which programs are appropriate for your camp, keeping in mind budget limits and the overall impact on your program. Finally, detail the cost savings and program benefits before you present your completed plan to your board of directors.

Worksheet 1–1 is designed to help you decide specifically which actions to take this year at camp. (Keep in mind your budget limits!)

Congratulations! You're on your way to a successful and rewarding season.

WORKSHEET 1–1
THE TOP-50 LIST OF ENVIRONMENTAL POSSIBILITIES

Do not try to do all, or even half, of these items. Any one item on this list will be enough to get you started. California's Brandeis-Bardin Institute's (BBI) camps tried to incorporate recycling, composting, energy and water management all at once. Though it accomplished great things, the price was a lot of friction. BBI officials admit they underestimated the magnitude of their commitment, as they did not prepare the way by slowly integrating the range of activities into their program.

The more you narrow your goals, the more likely you and your participants are to succeed. Remember: Today, you can do something. Tomorrow, you may be able to do everything.

Mark your responses: Y—yes, N—no, M—maybe.

Camp Infrastructure

_____ 1. Change shower heads to shut-off valve, low-flow units.

_____ 2. Repair leaks at all faucets.

_____ 3. Put water displacement bottles or dams in tank-style toilets.

_____ 4. Replace high-watt light bulbs with low-watt light bulbs.
　　　　　_____ indoors
　　　　　_____ outdoors

_____ 5. Install a gray water system for watering.

_____ 6. Install underground sprinklers with timers.

_____ 7. Install a solar unit to heat swimming pool.

_____ 8. Install a solar unit to heat indoor water.

_____ 9. Install a heat pump for heating/air-conditioning.

_____ 10. Upgrade furnace and air-conditioning to more efficient systems.

_____ 11. Check for leaks of chlorofluorocarbons (CFCs) such as freon and, if possible, replace with non-CFC units:
　　　　　_____ freezer
　　　　　_____ refrigerator
　　　　　_____ A/C units—buildings and vehicles

_____ 12. Replace pre-1979 fluorescent light fixtures that have PCBs in their ballasts.

_____ 13. Replace items that have asbestos.
　　　　　_____ ceiling tile
　　　　　_____ floor tile
　　　　　_____ pipe insulation sleeves
　　　　　_____ roofing tile
　　　　　_____ siding
　　　　　_____ consumer products

_____ 14. Take appropriate ventilation or other corrective action for buildings that contain radon.

_____ 15. Check age and disposition of any underground tanks.

_____ 16. Turn down water heater temperatures to 110°F. (The water heater feeding the kitchen's high-temp dishwasher may have to be kept at 130°F so as not to overwork the heat booster.)

_____ 17. Insulate and double-glaze windows in appropriate buildings.

_____ 18. Purchase nozzles for all hoses.

_____ 19. Use push brooms for deck and street cleaning instead of water hoses.

_____ 20. Establish a preventive maintenance schedule, including repair, lube, and tuning, for all camp equipment, machinery, and vehicles.

_____ 21. Purchase quality, long-life equipment. Teach staff and campers its value and how to maintain it.

_____ 22. Buy ceramic cups for all office personnel and staff to eliminate using disposable cups by the coffeemaker.

_____ 23. Buy rechargeable batteries for all battery-powered equipment.

Camp Procedures

_____ 24. Revamp ordering procedures to stock and use only products that are recyclable, biodegradable, and/or are shipped with a minimum of packaging.

_____ 25. Order in bulk when possible.

_____ 26. Eliminate or reduce hazardous materials—solvents, thinners, cleaning agents, oil-based paints, herbicides, pesticides, aerosols—wherever possible. Where not possible, check local regulations for handling, storing, and disposing of them.

_____ 27. Recycle or properly dispose of other hazardous wastes.

_____ 28. Machine-wash clothing in cold water, full loads only.

_____ 29. Dry clothes on lines instead of in automatic dryers.

_____ 30. Walk and use bicycles or tricycles around camp when possible.

_____ 31. Run only one out-of-camp trip per day to minimize vehicle use. Post an errand sheet on the office bulletin board so everyone can list what he or she need off-campus.

_____ 32. Coordinate camper transportation to and from camp and on field trips to minimize vehicle use.

_____ 33. Print on both sides of paper, and use back sides of envelopes, scrap paper and correspondence for notes.

_____ 34. Keep boxes by the computer printer and photocopy machine to collect mistakes for use as scrap paper.

_____ 35. Place extra collection bins in the cabins for aluminum and mixed paper as well as trash.

_____ 36. In the winter, clear walks with snow shovels instead of snow blowers. To clear ice, use sand or fireplace ash rather than rock salt.

Camp Projects and Experiential Education

_____ 37. Hold a weekly contest for best cabin at improving camp environment (e.g., least total garbage produced).

_____ 38. Ask campers and staff to carry water bottles or canteens for drinking.

_____ 39. Sell personal water bottles/canteens at the camp store so campers can fill at the tap or water fountain without wasting a drop of water.

_____ 40. Recycle office items such as paper, cardboard boxes, and newspapers.

_____ 41. Recycle items in the kitchen and around camp. Begin with aluminum, then add newspaper, cardboard, glass, and other miscellaneous materials.

_____ 42. Encourage campers to carry cloth handkerchiefs instead of disposable paper tissues.

_____ 43. Adopt a stream, lake, or other waterway near your camp to preserve as a nature study.

_____ 44. Escort insects out of your cabin; don't kill them.

_____ 45. Mount letter writing campaigns on environmental issues to legislators, public agencies, and private companies.

_____ 46. Conduct camp nature tours to teach guests about the local ecosystem.

_____ 47. Conduct tours of the camp garbage dumpster and hunt for recyclables (with proper supervision).

_____ 48. Plant a garden. (Plant seedlings in the ground one to two months before campers arrive if you have a summer-only program.)

_____ 49. Compost kitchen and yard wastes. Begin on a small scale with a worm bin, then graduate to larger-scale methods, such as hot piles and turning bins.

_____ 50. Teach campers and staff how to alert camp administrators to any environmental concerns.

2
PROGRAMMING

2
PROGRAMMING

"Environmentalists stress three Rs: reduce, reuse, recycle. But, there should be a fourth R—rethink—and it should come before the other three."
—New environmental litany

This chapter, written for camp directors and programmers, includes the building blocks for environmental programming for resident and day camps, along with suggested plans. You'll find adequate detail here to start your own environmental program, but you also should explore the resources listed in Appendix A. More good environmental curricula are being published today, and many of them are adaptable for camp use.

CREATING A PROGRAM OUTLINE

Programming Idea

Encourage your counselors and staff to help develop the environmental programming so they feel a sense of ownership in it. The more involved they feel, the harder they will work to make the programs succeed.

Successful programming treats every subject, old or new, in tempting and captivating ways. The following outline, designed by Santa Cruz, California-based programming expert Marla Cohen, helps you develop the foundation you need to capitalize on your creative environmental activities. Both day and resident camps can adapt most of the programs listed here.

A word of advice: before you begin developing your own environmental concepts, find out if the wheel has already been invented. Explore program banks at your own and related camps, and contact organizations such as ACA, 4-H, and the YMCA. Don't overlook books, either.

GOALS

Set two or three goals for your environmental program that answer the following questions. (Keep in mind what you want campers or staff members to say they learned.)

❑ What do I want to accomplish?
❑ Why am I offering this program?

Your goal statement might read like this: Over a period of five years, I'll establish a program that teaches environmental awareness skills that participants can use at home also.

OBJECTIVES

Set objectives for each goal (i.e., list how you intend to accomplish the goal), then write action steps to accomplish the objectives. Objectives for this example goal might include composting in the first year and recycling in the second year. Action steps then would include:

❑ Research composting and recycling methods, and choose the ones appropriate to my facility and program.
❑ Purchase equipment.
❑ Train the staff and get them excited about the activity.
❑ Schedule staff and composting activities appropriately (first year).
❑ Schedule staff and recycling activities appropriately (second year).

CAMP STRUCTURE

When you write your goals and objectives, you need to research how they fit into the existing camp structure. Answer the following questions. (You'll probably think of others as well.)

❑ Is this plan age-appropriate?
❑ How much time can our camp allot to this activity as a program in our day, week, or session?
❑ Can the facility accommodate this project or change?

FORMAT

If you decide the proposed activity will be part of the program, you need to determine how to present it. Ask yourself these questions about the program format, as you would with any new activity:

❑ Will campers participate through drama, games, writing, songs, skits, banner making, mural making, building, etc.?
❑ How can I integrate discussion into the program?
❑ What type of demonstrations and practice exercises are necessary?

PROGRAM PLAN

After you choose the format, you need to create the program. Ask yourself the following questions:

❑ How much time do I need to set up, run, wrap-up, and discuss the program?
❑ Who is participating? Which age groups?

❑ How, exactly, do I execute the program? (Provide details! Where do campers go? What do campers do? Include backup material, i.e., fact sheets.)

❑ How do I create an atmosphere or ambiance for the program? If it's a game, do I ham it up or find a host? Should I create musical and dramatic reading acts, make appropriate foods, sew costumes, hang art; or capitalize on a fad such as Sesame Street, the Simpsons, the Ninja Turtles, etc.?

MATERIALS NEEDED

From your program plan, list and evaluate all the materials you will need:

❑ Which props and how many?

❑ Where do I get these props?

❑ How long before the materials arrive?

❑ Is it cost-effective? If not, what can I substitute?

AVAILABLE RESOURCES

Next, make a list of every resource you have, or might have, at your disposal to make this program work:

❑ Day camps can use parents: encourage them to participate, and they will literally "take the lesson home."

❑ Day and resident camps can take advantage of outreach opportunities: partnering with charity organizations, senior adult centers or retirement homes, and local community activities, for example. This resource also demonstrates how campers easily can contribute to their communities after they return home.

EVALUATION

As with any new program, procedure, or policy, you must evaluate your efforts. Involve as many people as possible, including the campers and staff, to get an accurate picture.

❑ Ask: What was great about the program?

❑ Ask: How could this program be better?

❑ Write down the answers!

SAVE IT

Finally, add this success to your program bank, and recycle the idea!

SAMPLE DAILY SCHEDULES

The next step is to fit these activities into your camp's programming schedule. The simplest answer is to build them into the program as scheduled activities, or as a few minutes of work time after other activities.

Potential Pitfall

Avoid imposing programs and activities top-down (from the director or head staff to counselors and campers), even if you believe your ideas are fresher, more novel, and better than anyone else can conceive. Employees who are lower on the organizational chart tend to resist this tactic.

When creating schedules, remember your campers' ages. Is 45 minutes too long for their attention spans? Do you need to include a period after lunch for rest time or low-energy activities?

Also, consider altering your activity periods to allow enough time for composting and recycling actions, and then for travel to the next activity. Remember that smaller children have smaller feet and legs, so they may not move as quickly as you do. Campers and staff shouldn't feel rushed to get to the next period.

Consider these guidelines for resident and day camps:

RESIDENT CAMP SCHEDULE

7:30 A.M.   Wake-up.

7:45–8:30   Greet-the-day activity and prep, flag raising, announcements, line-up for breakfast.

8:30–9:15   Breakfast.

9:15–9:30   Recycling activities in kitchen. Allow 5 to 10 minutes to flatten boxes, rinse and store cans and bottles, collect compost materials, and feed the worm bin. Work schedule is arranged so KPs' cabinmates handle chores until the campers return from kitchen. If your camp composts on a small scale, composting chores can be completed within this 15-minute morning period. If your camp composts on a large scale, you have to assign two to four KPs for this task, and it will take 30 to 45 minutes. You may need two grounds crew members and a pickup truck to carry kitchen wastes to the composting area, also.

9:30–9:45   Cabin cleanup.

9:45–10:45   First activity period.

10:45–11:45   Second activity period.

11:45–Noon   Lunch prep, line-up for lunch.

Noon–12:45 P.M. Lunch.

12:45–1:45   Rest hour. KPs do recycling chores, then join others for rest hour. Compost should be mixed into outdoor hot piles or windrows only in the morning. So during lunch and dinner collect compost in garbage cans for delivery and mixing the following morning. This allows the natural decomposition process enough time to take effect before nightfall, when most rodents and predators come out to scavenge.

1:45–2:45   Third activity period.

2:45–3:45   Fourth activity period.

3:45–5:00   Free time, special activities.

5:00–5:30   Cleanup from special activities, prep for evening activities, dinner.

5:30–6:00   Flag lowering, ceremonies, announcements, line-up for dinner.

6:00–6:45   Dinner.

6:45–7:15   Continue prep for evening program while KPs do recycling, composting chores.

7:15–9:00   Evening program (incorporate ideas from later in this chapter).

9:00–9:30   Prep for bed.

9:30   Lights out.

DAY CAMP

7:00 A.M.–9:00   Morning child care (see below).

9:00–9:15   Greet-the-day circle: camp songs, announcements, special recognition to Eco-Patrols (EPs).

9:15–10:00   First activity period.

10:00–10:45   Second activity period.

10:45–11:30   Third activity period.

11:30–Noon   Group time.

Noon–12:30 P.M. Lunch.

12:30–12:45   Recycling. Have one person or group collect food waste as the Recycle and Compost Patrol (RC Patrol). Send all RCs with a counselor to worm bin, compost pile, recycling bins, etc.

12:45–1:30   Fourth activity period.

1:30–2:15   Fifth activity period.

2:15–3:00   Sixth activity period.

3:00–3:15   Snack.

3:15–3:30   Closing circle, announcements, and departures.

3:30–6:00   Afternoon child care (see below).

MORNING/AFTERNOON CARE

Every child care adapts to the varied ages of children, available site space, location, etc. One option is to organize environmental activities in stations that children can visit for self-guided, self-paced, or supervised activities. (You can also rotate stations through the day or week.) For example:

Station One: Reading: staff, children read alone.

Station Two: Arts and crafts: (1) stencil (a) endangered species on paper or notebooks with crayons or water paints; (b) different words, i.e., "Aluminum," "Glass," "Recycling," etc., for appropriate collection bins and collecting areas; (c) draw concepts such as the sun and the word "Solar," a plant and the word "Organic," etc.; (2) clay sculpture endangered species or local wildlife; (3) make murals of habitats and animals, healthy homes and cityscapes, etc.; (4) create flow charts of how toxic materials can pollute different resources and harm different animals.

Station Three: Garden-related activities: visit and stock the compost pile, turning bin, or worm bin; use composted soil for gardening; plant and/or harvest vegetables; learn to cook vegetables.

Station Four: Outside play area: Earthball, nature tours, search for forest animals, etc.

Station Five: Rest place: lie down in the grass or under a tree for quiet time.

A FIVE-SEASON PROGRAM SAMPLE

There are several ways to approach environmental themes for the camp season. Your camp's mission and available resources determine which specific environmental programs you create and adapt.

Marla Cohen suggests resident camps organize their programs around a five-year plan of environmental themes. For example, Season One might teach waste reduction; Season Two, water conservation; Season Three, energy conservation; Season Four, animals and their habitats; and Season Five, community action. By adding additional environmental programming each year, you give yourself time for appropriate planning and staff training, as well as entice your campers to return. The program for each theme year could include the following activities.

SEASON ONE: WASTE REDUCTION

The overall rethinking theme is: "Do you really need these products?" This season concentrates on reducing, reusing, recycling, and composting activities. Your curriculum should include inventories of personal and camp products; how to shop "smart" for products and packaging at stores; training about the care and maintenance of camp property; where to find the resources participants need for a waste-wise home; waste reduction Eco-Patrols; a toxics inventory and hazardous waste day; and garbage hoisting and weigh-in (see Chapter 3 for more information).

SEASON TWO: WATER CONSERVATION

The overall rethinking theme is: "Can you do it with less water?" Reduction activities should include turning off water while soaping in shower and brushing teeth, installing tank toilet water displacers and low-flow faucet heads, and fixing leaky faucets. Recycling efforts include using sink tubs of wash water with very little soap and five-gallon buckets of saved shower water to irrigate gardens and outdoor plants; and water-wise Eco-Patrols. If appropriate, add information on where to find the resources they need for a water-wise home; emphasize water-based media in art; and teach campers a rain dance (see Chapter 3 for more information).

SEASON THREE: ENERGY CONSERVATION

The overall rethinking theme is: "Can you do it with less energy?" Reduction activities include forming wattage-saver Eco-Patrols, and energy conservation resource investigators; and installing new bulbs, fixtures, lamps, and light switches. If appropriate, you can teach basic electricity and energy-wise shopping; take a power plant tour; construct a solar water-heater panel; cook with solar camp stoves; and detail where to find the resources they need for an energy-wise home (see Chapter 3 for more information).

SEASON FOUR: ANIMALS AND THEIR HABITATS

The overall rethinking theme is: "How can we share our space with animals?" Declare your camp a wildlife refuge; adopt a stream, pond, or wooded area (check with your state ecology or wildlife department, the National Wildlife Federation, or The Institute for Urban Wildlife for details); visit an aquarium, natural history museum or zoo; invite naturalists and foresters to speak; create a checklist of wildlife that lives in your area (check with Audubon Society and your state wildlife commission) and hike with binoculars to find them; refer to exercises in *Acclimatization, Sharing Nature With Children* and other manuals (see Appendix A for contact addresses).

SEASON FIVE: COMMUNITY ACTION

The overall rethinking theme is: "I can make a difference!" Participate in a community litter cleanup, recycling day, or retirement home activity, such as raking leaves for composting or installing low-wattage bulbs; promote a worthy environmental cause by going door to door in a neighborhood; write letters to American companies and political and public agency leaders expressing concern about specific environmental issues; write a children's environmental book; discuss how campers can make a difference when they return home (see Chapter 3 for more information).

This five-year program maintains program excitement in two ways: Repeat campers and counselors find something new each season. Also, by the sixth season—the first year you repeat a theme—the "old hands" campers can take leadership roles. During each camp session, you can offer groups of related programs and activities under the theme, introduce unrelated individual activities or elective activities, or both. You may wish to combine several themes such as energy and water conservation, and community action or habitats and waste management each year.

EQUIVALENTS

No doubt at some point in your program, you'll need to know how much recycled material equals which quantity of resources. This section covers most of the equivalents used in environmental programs.

All values are approximate. For example, when figuring the amount of energy saved in glass and steel recycling, industries use different types of furnaces (electric and gas-fired) with differing system efficiencies (old, which is less efficient, and new, which is more efficient), and different proportions of recycled material in several batches. For aluminum recycling, the energy consumed in recycling cans is so different from the energy for recycling aluminum foil, lawn chairs, or car parts that it's easier to give figures for the item consumers recycle most: aluminum beverage cans.

Thus, the following table contains the closest approximations currently available from the industries listed.

LIST OF EQUIVALENTS*

One tree

= 120 pounds of newsprint (a 4 to 6 months' daily subscription)

*Sources: American Paper Institute, New York, NY; Washington Natural Gas Co., Seattle, WA; Washington State Department of Ecology, Olympia, WA; Seattle City Light, Seattle, WA; Washington Natural Gas Co., Seattle, WA; Ball-Incon Glass Corp., Seattle, WA; Alcoa Aluminum Co., Pittsburgh, PA; The Steel Can Recycling Institute, Pittsburgh, PA.

One acre

>   = 43,560 square feet
>
>   = 435 trees (figuring a 10 foot x 10 foot plot of land, or 100 square feet, per tree)

640 acres

>   = one square mile
>
>   = 278,400 trees

Recycling one ton (2,000 pounds) of old paper into new paper instead of starting from scratch saves:

>   7,000 gallons of water
>
>   17 trees
>
>   682.5 gallons of power-plant oil
>
>   10,401 kilowatt hours (kwh)—enough to power an average home for six months
>
>   3.3 cubic yards of landfill
>
>   60 pounds of air pollutants

To light one 75–watt light bulb 24 hours a day for a year requires 657,000 watts of energy (657 kw). It takes the following energy sources to generate that 657 kw:

>   10,889 gallons of water through a dam's 30 megawatt (mw) hydro-electric generator (at 90 percent efficiency)
>
>   63 gallons of oil in an oil-fired power plant (at 30 percent efficiency)
>
>   516 pounds of coal in a coal-fired plant (at 35 percent efficiency)
>
>   59 cubic feet of gas in a natural gas-fired turbine plant (at 42 percent efficiency)

Manufacturers can save 657 kw when they make new products by recycling:

>   404 pounds of steel
>
>   102 pounds of aluminum beverage cans (per recycled can batch, vs. virgin material batch)
>
>   371 pounds of glass

1 kwh

>   = 3,413 Btu (British Thermal Units)

100,000 Btu

>   = 1 Therm (100K Btu)
>
>   = 1 cubic foot of natural gas
>
>   = 29.29 kwh
>
>   = 0.769 gallons of oil

DISCUSSION POINTS FOR SEMINARS AND EVENING PROGRAMS

If you choose to hold a discussion as part of your activities, be prepared with a list of discussion questions to add depth to the session. The following questions also work well for evening programs. Be sure to tailor these questions to your campers' age group.

❑ When you conserve, do you feel deprived? Why or why not?

❑ Which resources and products do you feel you deserve more of, and which can you make do with less? Do you think everyone in the world deserves as much of these resources as you do? Why or why not?

❑ By the time a typical American reaches the age of 70, he or she has generated approximately 600 times his weight in garbage. If you weigh 100 pounds, that means you'll leave about 60,000 pounds of trash for your children and grandchildren (from *The Recycler's Handbook*). How do you feel about that?

❑ You will probably use 1.3 million gallons of water during your lifetime (at the U.S. average of 50 gallons a day). How do you use that much water? Could you live comfortably with less than 50 gallons a day?

❑ Try to visualize the 51,000 pounds of food you will probably consume in your lifetime (at a lifetime average of two pounds a day). How much food do you waste?

❑ Can we truly save the natural resources on this planet, or should we just "party 'til it's over?"

❑ Scientists regularly warn us that by the year 2020, the Earth will run out of oil, coal and gas; 25 percent of our drinkable water may be polluted; the rainforests will be destroyed, taking away nearly half the planet's animal species and oxygen; and a huge hole will open in the ozone layer and toast the planet. At the same time, carbon dioxide gasses will enclose the planet, raise temperatures, melt the polar ice caps, and drown the continents. Do you believe these predictions? Why or why not? What positive signs and actions do you see that are counteracting these dire possibilities?

❑ Can our ingenuity and technology find solutions to clean up our environmental problems before things become desperate? Why or why not?

❑ Are you living in balance with nature? If so, how? If not, do you want to make any changes in your lifestyle? What changes?

❑ What motivates people to take action to solve an environmental problem?

❑ If you collected the world's 5.5 billion people in one place, and stood each one in a space two feet square, they would only occupy 818 square miles, (a square 28.6 miles x 28.6 miles), about the size of a medium-sized U.S. city. Compared to the size of the Earth, people are as small as ants. Why do we overwhelm all of this giant planet's resources?

❏ Did you know that, barring catastrophic war and/or disease, our planet's population could *double* in just over 20 years, *double again* in 20 more years, and *double again 20 years later*. By the year 2050, there could be over 40 billion humans on Earth. Can the planet support this many people? Do we want to find out?

❏ Where did we come from, and why do we continue to survive?

❏ The latest celestial discovery (in 1992) is gaseous patterns in distant galaxies, supporting the scientific theory that our universe was started with a "Big Bang." What came before the "Bang," and before the gas clouds?

❏ Do humans live at an arbitrary point in the evolution of life on this planet? Do you think the process will continue beyond our point?

❏ Our nomadic ancestors followed the game and plants in their territory through the seasons without carrying many possessions. Imagine you are a nomad that has to live on whatever you can carry on your back or in your car. What would you choose to take with you on your travels? How would you treat the earth, plants, and animals if you knew you were always coming back to the same places?

❏ Should we believe every "green" or "ecological" message we read on packages, and hear about on commercials?

❏ If "recyclable" is printed on a package, does that mean you can actually recycle it where you live, camp, go to school, or work?

❏ If "natural" is printed on a product, what does it mean?

❏ If plastic is labeled "biodegradable," is that true?

❏ What are consumer corporations (that is, companies that manufacture foodstuffs, clothing, electronics, tools, etc.) doing to reduce the waste they generate? Would you still buy your favorite group's CD if you knew the packaging company was wasteful?

❏ What are these corporations doing to help you reduce the waste you generate?

❏ If only a few people use a resource, can there still be a shortage of that resource? If your camp drew its water from a lake, would it be okay for you to use all the water? Why or why not?

❏ If you are the only one in the forest, is it okay for you to use all the trees? Why or why not?

❏ How much value do you put on people that will come after you? Next session? Next year? Your children in 20 years?

BEYOND PROGRAMMING

The following suggestions detail actions and items you can build into your camp routines without specific programming. Realize that you can get "extra mileage" in terms of parental good will, public recognition, possible income, and support from your board if you attract local newspapers and magazines to write about your programs.

❏ At camp pre-registration, sell T-shirts and sweatshirts that say, "I recycle at _____ Camp," or "I help the earth at _____ Camp."

❑ At camp registration, sell "earth-wise" items with your camp logo/ name printed on them: reusable shopping bags, lunch bags and boxes (in metal, nylon, plastic, or canvas), water bottles and carrying belts, to name a few. Try to get water bottles made from recycled plastic— they're available at bicycle, toy, convenience, and auto supply stores, and from wholesalers. These items identify the user as a participant or supporter of your camp wherever they lunch, shop, bicycle, etc. You may even offer these items as gifts to full-paid participants.

❑ At camp registration, offer packages of five cloth napkins (one for each day of the week) at reduced rate for early or full-paid registrants. Campers can crayon batik or tie-dye them as a camp art project; parents can launder them at end of week.

❑ At the camp store, sell recycled paper products: camp stationery, note pads, postcards, etc., printed on recycled paper.

❑ Encourage parents to buy products made from recycled materials and send earth-wise products to camp with their children.

❑ Sell *50 Things Kids Can Do To Save The Earth* through your canteen or bookstore (see Appendix A for publisher information).

❑ Create picnic baskets filled with reusable items for sale or raffle.

❑ Ask parents to pack lunch items in reusable plastic containers or recyclable foil instead of with plastic film. (If they include a napkin, it should be cloth, not paper.) Also, suggest they not pack whole fruit— children rarely finish more than half a piece of fruit.

❑ Try this experiment with campers: Prepare a letter for parents informing them that for the first day or two of camp, you'll ask campers to repack what they don't eat in their lunches, and take it home. Parents can understand immediately how much their children eat and how much they waste, and what they do and do not like. Explain that by planning what they send to camp with their children, they help reduce the camp's trash, and the expenses for hauling it away. Follow-up with phone calls, letters, or environmental awareness certificates to thank parents and let them know their efforts are appreciated.

❑ Use food scraps from camp lunches for worm composting (see Chapter 7 for more information).

❑ Use metal flatware for picnics instead of plastic. To clean, run it through your facility's dishwasher. The metal flatware can be purchased cheap at thrift stores. If you must buy plastic, plan to wash and reuse it, too. Should your facility lack a dishwasher, use paper plates and cups that can be torn up and composted or thrown out with little environmental impact.

FINAL THOUGHTS

An effective environmental program for your campers starts with a well-conceived plan. Begin by developing a five-year schedule for implementing environmental themes. Next, outline the steps you need to take to accomplish these plans. Finally, write out a specific time schedule, allotting extra time for campers to complete the environmental tasks.

Creativity and imagination are the keys to programming success. Don't hesitate to add interesting facts on how much energy your campers are saving, or ask them thought-provoking questions. You may gain new programming ideas from their responses!

3
ENVIRONMENTAL ACTIVITIES

"Tell me and I will forget;
Show me and I may remember;
Involve me and I will understand."
—Chinese proverb

START BY RETHINKING

Now that you have developed an environmental philosophy and a program outline, you must develop activities that reinforce new ways for you and your campers to treat your ecosystem. In other words you need to rethink.

There are a thousand and one activities to accomplish this thought process. Start with the rethinking themes listed in the Seasons guidelines in Chapter 2. You can branch out and add the activities detailed in this chapter. The sections cover materials waste, energy and water conservation, animals, toxic waste handling, and community involvement.

In each of the eight categories presented in this section, focus on cooperation and discovery. None of these activities is intended as a policing action or as a competition, unless it is a friendly one where everyone learns something new. However, you may want to create an awards system, such as a certificate of completion for each activity or a reward certificate for special accomplishments.

This is only a sampling of the activities from which to build your environmental program. There are thousands more in other books and in use in programs like yours. Refer to the reading list in Appendix A, and talk with other programmers to discover their favorite activities.

BIG PICTURE ACTIVITIES

The ideas in this section help campers visualize the big picture, environmentally speaking, and their place in that picture. Adapt activities and discussion questions to fit your ecosystem, camp facility, and camper age group.

While camp may seem like an island from the inside, everyone can see from the outside that it must interact with the rest of its ecosystem to survive. Rabbi Bob Davis, director of camping and youth programs at Shwayder Camp in Colorado, suggests taking campers and counselors physically out of camp to a vantage point where they can see it in the context of its surroundings.

For example, you might take campers to the other side of the lake so they can see the camp in relationship to the private homes on the same shore. In addition, have campers study maps of the area to help them visualize where the camp is relative to nearby towns that serve the camp's needs. Or talk about a river that flows through your camp: Does the water flow through camp or town first? Does it matter?

Why not take everyone out to stargaze at night? Remind campers that most of the stars they see are part of a solar system like ours. Imagine beings on those other worlds struggling with the same kinds of environmental problems we have. Ask campers, "If you flew to these galaxies as a consultant from Earth, how would you help them solve their environmental problems?"

Math/computer teacher Jeff Strickler, at the Northwest School in Seattle, Washington, uses this puzzle to get his students thinking about humans' impact on the environment: Imagine a lake where algae grows. Every minute, the algae population doubles. In 60 minutes, the lake is completely covered. At what point will the lake be half covered? (Answer: minute 59). And only 25 percent covered? (Answer: minute 58). Right until its last two minutes, most of the lake is open territory. Today, environmentalists are warning that we humans have come to our "last two minutes" on Earth.

To bring this discussion closer to home, have campers take a look at the environmental changes happening locally. Identify the type of ecosystem where you and your campers are located: boreal, tropical or coastal forest, chaparral, sage desert, steppe, mountain, prairie, mixed forest, deciduous forest, or everglade. Then identify which trees, grasses, weeds and shrubs, animals, and insects share this ecosystem. Finally, ask campers to reflect on their discoveries: Are all the plants you see at camp native to this ecosystem? Have humans introduced any plants to this ecosystem that are now causing problems for the native plants? Are any of the animals you expect in this climate zone missing? Why? Do you see any you didn't expect?

MANAGING MATERIALS AND SOLID WASTE

The activities in this section will enable each participant to put the values of recycling and composting in perspective, and they'll create more overall interest for solid waste management.

GARBAGE HOISTING

Garbage hoisting is a great activity to reinforce how much trash campers produce in a day. The goals are for them to think before they waste during camp, then practice this awareness at home. (This program can be adapted to work for any age group in day or residence camps.)

You'll need the following supplies:

❑ Plastic garbage bags or paper grocery sacks,

❑ Pencil/pen and paper for recording,

❑ Scale for weighing garbage.

GARBAGE HOISTING ACTIVITY ONE At the beginning of the day, give each staff member and camper (or camper unit) a plastic bag. Ask campers and staff members to put every single thing they'd normally throw out during the day (except toilet paper) in their bag. Have them carry their bag from activity to activity. They'll soon be dragging arts and crafts waste, snack wrappers, soda cans, and lunch leftovers. Do not allow recycling and composting during the first day.

At the end of the first day, weigh the bags to see how much trash each person (or unit) generated. At the same time, record the types of trash—paper, plastic, food, metals—that were collected, and note which material appeared most often.

Have campers repeat the garbage hoisting activity on the second day to see if they can generate less trash. If they reduce their waste output, allow them to explore other options for handling the remaining waste, such as reducing what they buy or collect, reusing the products, recycling, or composting.

GARBAGE HOISTING ACTIVITY TWO At the end of the first week of camp, take the campers and staff to the camp dumpster. Have them peer over the upwind edge (to reduce the smell), and observe the materials that have been discarded. Discuss the contents of the dumpster with campers:

❑ Which materials are reusable, recyclable, or compostable?

❑ What are these materials worth, and why do we give them this value?

❑ How effective would composting and recycling be in reducing this particular solid waste output?

❑ Remind them to think before they throw away items.

GARBAGE HOISTING ACTIVITY THREE Again, issue garbage bags to campers and staff, and stage a contest to see which group or camper can generate the least amount of trash over a period of days or one week. Tell them they may use any of the four Rs, but they cannot dump trash elsewhere just to win. Weigh the bags at the end of each day and discuss the contents using the questions in Activity Two.

CARPENTRY 101

The goal of this activity is to help campers better understand resource use and waste by creating new objects from "junk" around your camp. Hopefully, like the garbage hoisting activity, campers will take these principles to heart at home, too.

You'll need the following supplies and preparation:

❑ Make a list of the "waste" materials available at your camp (#10 cans, scrap paper, scrap lumber, extra window screening, etc.).

❑ Tour the camp, and discuss with staff which objects need repair, which items need to be built, and what your campers could create as part of a charity or community project in the area. Possibilities include foot stools, book shelves, bins for worm composting, trellises, plaques, and filing bins.

❑ From that discussion, prepare a list of projects that use your available waste materials. Include time requirements, age appropriateness, technical level, safety risks, and a list of the appropriate materials and necessary tools in your plan.

❑ Brief staff on the projects' goals and objectives.

❑ Allow staff members to select a specific project from your list. Let members determine how much time to schedule for their individual projects.

❑ Have a sign-up sheet ready. Each counselor's name should appear on the sheet with space to record which project he or she wishes to do and expected day of completion.

❑ Set up an orientation meeting so staff and campers can discuss their project with maintenance and other resource staff.

Inform the campers that the camp needs some repairs, new objects, and donations for the local community. Explain that the camp units (or another grouping) will design pre-chosen objects using "junk" materials around the camp (i.e., a piece of art such as a sculpture, mural, painting, etc., or a utilitarian item such as a chair, table, bookcase, toy, or utensil). Each group will complete its design by the specified deadline and objects will be approved by the appropriate maintenance or resource staff person.

As each group completes its project, be sure to inform the rest of the camp. If the object can be displayed in a communal meeting place, do so. If not, encourage groups to tour the site.

Whenever possible, take photographs of both the work in progress and the finished piece. This documents the projects for parents, for the camp newsletter, and for outside publicity to newspapers, camp magazines, businesses, and state and federal representatives. Publicity also encourages continued local and parent support for future camp environmental education programs.

ADDITIONAL SOLID WASTE MANAGEMENT ACTIVITIES

Here are additional activities you may want to try at your camp. Many of these can be successfully combined with the garbage hoisting and carpentry programs.

❏ Ask each camper and staff person to make a chart of their personal effects inventory, checking off which items they can do without, which they can reuse, which they can recycle, which they must throw away at some point, and which have more packaging than necessary for the product. For example, a pair of old jeans might fall into categories one, two, and three. Discuss how to take care of items that will be reused.

❏ Ask campers and staff to do an inventory of camp products, and list which the camp needs for the program, which it doesn't, which can be reused or recycled, which eventually must be thrown away, and which have more packaging than necessary. Discuss how to take care of items that will be reused.

❏ Call your local solid waste department and trash hauler to learn which recyclable materials they accept, and how to collect and recycle these items. Then start participating in the local program.

❏ Start a basic recycling program at camp, accepting items that require little work, such as cardboard boxes (flatten), aluminum and steel cans (rinse in a bucket of water rather than under a running tap, then crush), glass and plastic (rinse), newsprint, and office paper.

❏ Install an inexpensive, wall-mounted can crusher so campers can compact their aluminum soda and juice cans for your limited storage space.

❏ Inform parents in writing that the camp is recycling. Detail which products you handle, and ways they can help, i.e., by packing lunches appropriately (see lunch preparation in Chapter 2 for more information).

❏ Arrange a field trip to a recycling facility to explain how your camp's recyclables are used after they leave your storage area.

❏ Participate in a plastics collection day at local supermarkets or with another local youth organization.

❏ Do a composting demonstration pile or turning bin with landscape trimmings and grass clippings. (Schedule this as a morning or afternoon activity; see Chapter 9.)

❏ If you operate from a building that is surrounded by maintained landscape, start a holding or turning bin to compost its grass clippings and leaves. (Schedule this as a morning or afternoon activity; see Chapter 9.)

❏ Build a worm bin, and feed the red worms with food scraps from campers' lunches. The bin can take a pound of food per square foot of surface area per week. Schedule extra KPs and time after breakfast for any composting activity that involves adding food stuffs to the compost pile. Food stuffs should be added to compost piles, bins, and trenches only in the morning so the natural decomposition can be underway by nightfall. This will keep rodents from the compost and limit presence of insects.

❏ Award certificates to the campers for good waste management ideas.

❏ Post campers' good waste management ideas on the bulletin board or in the camp newsletter.

(See Chapters 7, 8, and 9 for worksheets and more information on these subjects.)

ENERGY CONSERVATION

When considering energy and water conservation activities, it's best to begin with simple projects such as turning down water heater temperatures and changing to lower-wattage light bulbs. Before proceeding, however, present these ideas to the facility's owner or manager, with the assurance that the changes will save money, and make you a more satisfied customer if you rent your facility.

You can easily structure the activities in this section to work for day camps as well as resident camps. Simply inform day-camp parents about the project, have campers apply the activities at home, then ask parents to send samples of their household electric bills before and after the conservation efforts. (Parents should white-out or cross out their names and addresses on bills.) Congratulate households which make energy-wise changes with certificates for children and parents.

WATT HUNTERS

The watt hunters activity acquaints campers with basic electricity ideas and teaches them where to find and how to install household products and equipment.

After completing this fun assignment, participants should understand how to save energy, both at camp and at home through simple tasks.

You'll need the following supplies and preparation:

❏ Create a checklist of camp electrical items. For example:

ITEM	HOW MANY? ×	WATTS EACH ×	HOURS OF DAILY USE =	WATT HOURS
cabin light bulbs	_____	_____	_____	_____
latrine light bulbs	_____	_____	_____	_____
mess hall light bulbs	_____	_____	_____	_____
air conditioners	_____	_____	_____	_____
Total (1,000 Watt hours = 1 kwh)				_____

❏ Make copies of the checklist for each camper group.

❏ Gather pencils and clipboards to record wattages and calculate totals.

❏ Provide one calculator per group.

❏ Bring a camp utility bill to the activity.

❏ Gather catalogs of energy-saving electrical equipment (such as *Real Goods* or *Seventh Generation*: see Appendix A).

❏ Make a list of the wattage figures on outdoor lamps and other hard-to-access items that require electricity such as camp computers, monitors and printers, freezers and refrigerators, radios and televisions, etc.

❏ Learn the price the camp pays for energy from each utility.

WATT HUNTERS ACTIVITY Note: This activity requires a fairly well-developed attention span and math skills.

Form pairs of campers to count and record the wattages of light bulbs, machines, and appliances around camp. Each group can inventory all electric appliances, or campers can inventory appliances in assigned areas. Wattages are printed on the globe of each bulb; machine wattages are located on serial number plates. Have counselors direct the wattage audit, then meet back at a central location at a specified time.

If lighting is the same in each cabin, campers can count one cabin's bulbs and water heater (if there is one), and multiply that number by the number of cabins at camp to get a total figure. To that, add the wattages of computers and printers, televisions and radios, kitchen appliances, motors, hot water heaters (if electric), washing machines, dryers (if electric), etc., to that cabin wattage total.

When the pairs gather again, have each team present its numbers to calculate how often the camp uses each light or machine every day. Utility companies measure power consumption in kilowatt hours, or kwh; every 1,000 watts you use equals a kilowatt. Ask campers, "How much energy does our camp use, in kwh, every day? How much do you think this costs?" Show a camp utility bill, then ask, "How much energy do you think your family uses at home?"

Pass out the catalogs, and ask campers to find high-efficiency light bulbs to replace those the camp now uses. Note how much less wattage these items use (up to 90% less), how much longer they last than regular light bulbs (about 10,000 hours), and their prices. Now, check newspaper ads or call a discount store, and ask how much regular bulbs, which last 750 to 1,000 hours, cost.

Next, using the numbers for the energy-saving bulbs, calculate in kwh how much electricity the camp would use if it had the new bulbs. Ask campers to report any savings.

Calculate how much it would cost to buy energy-saving bulbs for every camp light fixture, compared to older style bulbs. Determine how many old bulbs it takes to give as many hours' light as a new, energy-efficient bulb. Multiply that number by the price of the old bulbs to get the total cost of older style bulbs.

Now, calculate how many times each older bulb must be changed, compared to how many times you'll change an energy-saving one. Determine how many minutes each older light bulb change takes. Multiply that number of minutes by the total number of changes for old light bulbs. Ask campers, "Is someone at camp paid to change light bulbs? How much does that person earn per hour?" Multiply their answers, then calculate the cost to change the newer bulbs only once.

Add the following calculations in this energy exercise:

The camp's total dollar cost of energy (the kwhs).

+ The total dollar cost to change older light bulbs.

+ The total dollar cost for older light bulbs.

Total $_____

Then add:

The total dollar cost of new bulbs.

+ The total dollar cost in energy for the new bulbs.

+ The total dollar cost to change the new bulbs one time.

Total $_____

Have campers compare the totals, and discuss how they can figure similar totals at home, too.

ADDITIONAL ENERGY CONSERVATION ACTIVITIES

❑ Build a solar water-heater panel (see Appendix A for plan sources).
❑ Build an outdoor solar shower (the sun heats water stored in a hanging, water-tight bag with a shut-off shower head at bottom end).
❑ Cook on a solar stove or in a solar oven.
❑ Deputize campers as Eco-Patrollers, or EPs.
❑ Arrange field trips to the local power plant to learn more about power sources, how the utilities conserve power, and what they suggest communities can do to help. Plants generally hand out conservation literature and kits for their "VIP" tourists to use at home.
❑ Find lights, heaters, machines, air conditioners, etc., that have been left on, and turn them off. Give certificates to everyone for saving energy.
❑ Have campers help install new light bulbs, photovoltaic switches, motion sensors, dimmers, solar lights, and other energy-saving items throughout the camp.
❑ Use cold water to wash and rinse hands, laundry, dishes, etc. when possible.
❑ Set up a clothesline for drying laundry.
❑ Award certificates to campers with good energy conservation ideas and families that incorporate the ideas at home.
(See Chapter 5 for worksheets and more information on this subject.)

WATER CONSERVATION

These activities, like the ones for energy conservation, work for day camps and resident camps. Again, inform day-camp parents of your efforts, have campers apply the strategies at home, then ask parents to provide before and after water bills for comparison at camp. Congratulate children and parents who make water-wise changes at home.

WATER WORKS

The goals of these activities are to teach campers how to save water through simple tasks and apply those skills at camp and at home.

ACTIVITY ONE: TOILET-TANK DISPLACER PROJECT You'll need the following supplies:

❏ Empty 1-liter or 2-liter plastic soda or juice bottles and caps in sizes that fit the camps' toilet tanks,

❏ Pebbles,

❏ Water,

❏ Wire,

❏ Pliers,

❏ A 4-cup measure or siphon hose,

❏ A 5-gallon bucket marked in one-gallon increments.

Divide campers into groups, with at least one counselor leading each group. Have a group go to the first toilet, pull off the top of tank, note the water level, and use a 4-cup measure or siphon to empty the tank's water into the bucket. Explain this is how much water goes down the drain with every flush. Next, ask campers to fill appropriate-sized soda bottles with pebbles and water, and place one securely in each toilet tank. Pour water from the bucket back into the tank until the earlier water level has been reached. The remaining water in the bucket is the amount of water saved by the bottle with each flush. At four flushes per day, how much water does the bottle save per season? Per year?

Replace the tank cover. Have groups repeat the previous step at each tank toilet around camp.

ACTIVITY TWO: SHOWER HEAD PROJECT In this activity, campers learn how to save water by installing a low-flow shower head in the bathroom.

You'll need the following supplies:

❏ Paper and pencils,

❏ Low-flow, or aerator, shower heads,

❏ Teflon tape,

❏ Adjustable wrenches,

❏ Five-gallon buckets marked in one-gallon increments,

❏ A camp water utility bill, or knowledge of the price per gallon the camp pays for water.

Organize a team of older campers, with a counselor leader heading each group, to help replace the camp's shower heads with low-flow models. Have campers run one shower with an older style shower head into the bucket for one minute. Measure and record the amount of water collected. Ask campers to pour collected water on a shrub or tree, then return.

Now, replace the old head with a new aerator head. Run water into the bucket for one minute, then again measure and record the amount collected. Note the number of gallons saved per minute per shower. Have campers multiply this savings by the number of showers in camp to calculate the total number of gallons you'd save per minute if every shower were in use. Then, suggest campers calculate the dollar savings to the camp, based on the camp's per-gallon water cost. (You can figure savings over time by multiplying the gallons per minute by the number of minutes it takes the average camper to shower. Multiply this total by the number of campers; multiply that figure by number of showers each camper takes in a week, and so on.)

Ask campers, "Based on these activities, how much water do you think your family uses each day in the shower? What are other ways to control this waste?"

ACTIVITY THREE: WATER ECO-PATROL This activity teaches campers to recognize water-wasting activities and take responsibility for resolving the situation.

You'll need the following supplies:

❑ Paper and pencils,

❑ Containers with volume marks (pint, quart, gallon), as appropriate to item being measured (you'll need a smaller container to measure water use at a sink or drinking fountain than at a shower).

Divide campers into Eco-Patrol teams to measure how much water is wasted by leaving water running while soaping in the shower, brushing teeth, and drinking from a fountain and through leaking faucets and showers. To determine the latter, follow the steps below. Remember, do not make this a policing action, but rather, a voyage of discovery where everyone is a winner for saving water.

1. Carry a 4-cup measure as you tour the campsite, watching for leaky faucets everywhere.

2. When you find a leaky faucet, place the cup under the leak, and time the drip for 30 seconds—which should yield enough water in the cup to measure.

3. Multiple the time and the volume by 2 to get the amount for 1 minute. (For instance, if you got a half-cup in 30 seconds, your faucet is leaking 1 cup per minute.)

4. Multiple both time and volume by 60 again to figure the amount leaking in 1 hour.

5. Continue to multiply by hours per day and days per session to get total water wasted per session.

Another option is for camp maintenance personnel to take the Eco-Patrol campers along when replacing washers and fixing faucets.

ADDITIONAL WATER WORKS ACTIVITIES

The following suggestions can be used separately, or in conjunction with the other conservation activities detailed in this chapter:

❑ To help campers visualize how much water is available for human use, fill a dishtub with water, and ask them to imagine it's the 385,000,000,000,000 (almost four-hundred trillion) gallons scientists say exist on Earth. Now, pour out 98 percent of the water—that's the salt water, which can't be used as drinking water. Now, throw out half of the remaining 2 percent of water in the bucket, because half of our potential drinkable water is frozen in polar ice caps. Now, to represent the Earth's human population, drop a handful of sand in the remaining water.

By dividing, we see that each one of the 5.5 billion people on Earth gets 635 gallons at any point in the Earth water (hydrologic) cycle—enough to last Americans, who use an average of about 53 gallons a day per person, one month. Ask campers: Name ways you could save water during the day. Would you use less water if you had to fetch it from a public well in heavy buckets, as people in many of the world's less-developed countries do?

❑ Test your camp's sprinkler watering efficiency. Gather a 5–gallon bucket with 1–gallon increments marked on it, a stopwatch or a watch with a sweep second hand, and three empty cans. Turn on the hose full blast and measure how much water pours into the bucket in 30 seconds. Have campers multiply the measurement by two to determine the flow rate of your water line in gallons per minute.

Next, attach a sprinkler to the hose and place it in the middle of an open space. Turn on the sprinkler for a minute, then measure and record the area of ground its spray covers, in square feet.

Mark the inside of three empty cans at 3/4 inch from the bottom, and place them at various distances from your sprinkler. Again, turn on the water, noting the exact time. Every few minutes, check the cans to see how fast they are filling. As the water reaches the mark on each can, recheck the time. Ask campers: How long did it take to fill the closest can? The middle can? The farthest can? Add their answers to these three questions. Divide the total by three to determine the average length of time your camp should water the grass.

Finally, multiply the average time in minutes by the gallons per minute coming from your water line (your first figure in this exercise). This tells campers how many gallons it takes to efficiently water the area your sprinkler covers.

❑ Have campers help install drip irrigation and soaker lines in gardens, orchards, flower and shrub beds. These lines enable you to soak the ground around your plants gradually, not wasting sprayed water elsewhere, as sprinklers do. Contact your local nursery, water

A Closer Look

Plants and creatures do have enough fresh water to survive on Earth, thanks to the hydrologic cycle, in which water evaporates from the planet, forms clouds, then returns as rain, snow, or hail. Our planet stores water on mountains in snow packs, which melt to form streams and rivers, and in underground caverns, called aquifers, where the surface water percolates down, leaving its impurities in the rock as it passes through. You can see this when you visit caves, and witness the water dripping from the rock ceiling.

department, or county extension agent to learn where to get these lines, and how to place them most effectively for irrigation. Junior high to adult participants can handle laying the lines.

❏ Have campers help with xeriscaping, or drought-tolerant landscaping. Generally, people double their water use in summer, when they water their lawns, gardens, and shrubs to keep them green. Landscaping with native species that are acclimatized to local summers reduces or eliminates that need to water. Call your local nursery or county extension agent to learn which plants are most drought-tolerant for your climate zone. Allow older youth-group participants to make the phone calls, then select and purchase the plants for landscaping at a youth center or local nursing home as a special project.

❏ Encourage campers to carry plastic drinking bottles (preferably the ones your camp sells) they can fill at taps and drinking fountains without wasting a drop.

❏ Find leaky faucets and fountains, running hoses, etc., and turn them off or repair them. Give certificates to everyone for saving water.

❏ Tour the local dam, reservoir, or water pumping station to answer the question, "Where does our water come from?"

❏ Learn a rain dance; contact your local Native American Resource Center to ask if any experts are available to relate the historical significance of the dance and teach the movements.

❏ Invite a water hunter to demonstrate how he or she uses a "water witch," or a well-digger, and talk about locating underground sources.

❏ Adopt a stream, pond, or beach that campers can help keep clean. (Contact your local or state environment department about adoption programs.) Learn the water source for your adopted area, what lives in it, what affects its flow, and how humans can help keep it healthy.

HABITATS AND ANIMALS

The activities in this section help campers appreciate how a community interacts, and how humans can exist in it and still keep it healthy.

TREASURE HUNT ACTIVITY

This activity acquaints participants with your camp's biotic community: its climate, animals, and plants. Participants also will sharpen their observation skills and learn to research the ecosystems in which they live.

Note: For any activity in a natural area, remind participants that this is home to the creatures who live there. Participants should stay on existing paths; refrain from picking plants, leaves, and flowers; and create as little impact on the natural area as possible.

You'll need the following supplies and preparation:

❏ One set of binoculars for each group of campers,

❏ Checklists,

❏ Pencils or pens for checking off animal, bird, insect, and plant sightings,

❏ Water bottles for hikes.

❏ Contact your state fish and wildlife department, county extension agent, or local Audubon Society to learn which climate zone your camp is located in, and which plants, animals, and insects are native to this general zone, and your particular area.

❏ Create a checklist of the most prominent animals, birds, insects, and plants in the area; don't forget to describe these items as well. Make enough copies (both sides of paper) for all staff and campers.

Once you arrive at the designated nature area, give campers a copy of the checklist and have them check off each species as they spot it. Direct them along a pre-marked trail or suggest areas where they will most likely spot the insects, animals, and plants. This activity could be part of a games-day team competition, although it's likely the commotion of a games day will scare animals away. You might accomplish your goal quicker if you send campers on the treasure hunt as a simple non-competitive hike during an activity period. At the end of the time period, walk as a group along the path and have participants point out the species they found. Discuss where the species live and why they live there, what they eat, their purpose in the ecosystem, and how they interrelate. Give certificates to everyone for respecting the camp's ecosystem.

TREASURE HUNT VARIATION On a standard hike, carry binoculars and "deputize" each participant as a climate zone investigator. Have the group hunt for the listed insects, animals, and plants, and call them out (softly so as not to scare other wildlife away) as they see them.

ADDITIONAL HABITATS AND ANIMALS ACTIVITIES

The following suggestions can be used separately or in conjunction with other conservation activities:

❏ Contact your local bird feed store or garden shop nursery, and learn which flowers, foods, and housing opportunities attract the birds in your climate zone. Have campers put out bird feeders and observe which birds come to eat.

❏ Build birdhouses with different-sized entrance holes, and observe which birds come to nest.

❏ Plant appropriate flowering plants, and observe which insects and birds are attracted to them.

❏ Declare your camp a Wildlife Sanctuary. Contact your state wildlife department or National Wildlife Federation to get application forms (see Appendix A).

❏ Invite a representative from the Audubon Society, outdoor club, local extension service, or state fish and wildlife department to "show and tell" how habitat changes affect all animals from penguins in Antarctica to deer, rabbits, and owls in American and European forests.

❑ Adopt a stream, pond, or forest area. Learn which animals live in the ecosystem, how they interact, and how humans can help keep their homes healthy.

❑ Take a field trip to your local aquarium and zoo to see animals from your ecosystem. Learn how they behave, what their young look like (petting areas are effective in building child-animal relationships), and what type of foods and shelter they need to survive.

HAZARDOUS MATERIALS

The activities in this section teach campers how to recognize and eliminate or find substitutes for the hazardous materials they use at camp and home. (Note: You should explain these activities to parents before proceeding to assure them of their children's safety.)

HAZARDOUS MATERIALS INVENTORY

Refer to Chapter 4 for the basic list of hazardous materials categories. As an activity, divide participants into groups, and give them copies of the list. Then ask them to find any products in their cabins and around camp that fall into each category, or assign each team to cover a particular area. Reconvene later, or the next day, and discuss what each team has found. Which of the products are necessary to functions at the camp? Which products are not necessary and can be eliminated? For which products can safer alternatives be substituted? You may wish to do this activity with the participation of a representative or expert from a local public environmental agency or consulting firm (see below).

Call your local solid waste department to learn where you can dispose of hazardous materials. Invite a speaker from that site or from a hazardous materials company to "show and tell" how to handle and dispose of the materials. (If appropriate, take a field trip to the hazardous waste disposal facility.) Afterwards, discuss products that can be substituted for toxics.

Finally, have campers prepare a list of the environmentally friendly products available in your locality to replace hazardous materials (see Appendix A for catalog resources).

HAZARDOUS WASTE DAY

Arrange with your solid waste department to set up a specific morning or afternoon to collect hazardous materials from parents, friends, and neighbors of your day camp. More than half of household toxics you will collect probably will be paint. If a large enough quantity of that paint is fresh, save it to use for projects at camp.

You also can have your camp participate in a local disposal site. Resident camps could have staff and campers inventory the camp for hazardous materials and collect unnecessary products. Deliver these to the disposal site.

ADDITIONAL HAZARDOUS-MATERIAL ACTIVITIES

❏ Make stencils campers can use to paint messages at storm drains on roads around the camp's neighborhood. Messages might include: "Don't Dump Waste Here," or "This Leads to the Lake."

❏ Arrange a tour of a hazardous waste disposal site, so campers can learn how the authorities dispose of these items.

WRITING PROJECTS

Writing is one of the most effective tools you can hand campers to foster environmental awareness in their communities. The activities in this section outline specific writing projects and suggestions to fire your campers with contagious enthusiasm.

EFFECTIVE LETTER WRITING

This activity provides opportunities for campers to exert their influence and build writing skills through letter writing campaigns to businesses and elected officials.

You'll need to do the following preparations:

❏ Choose one environmental issue, then create a fact sheet about it. Make sure you have your facts straight and can explain the issue simply enough for campers to write a coherent letter.

❏ List the facts on a board or large pad of paper so campers can refer to them as they write.

❏ Prepare self-addressed (campers' home addresses) stamped envelopes so the company or legislator can write them back.

Ask campers to write a letter in their own words about environmental issues. If they are stuck for ideas on what to write and/or to whom to address their letters, suggest these possibilities:

❏ Tell your mayor or legislator about your camp's environment programs and how you wish the rest of the city, county, state and/or country did the same.

❏ Ask a company to use more recyclable packaging.

❏ Ask a fast-food company to start composting.

❏ Compliment legislators, bureaucrats, businesses, agencies, clubs, and parents who have a positive impact on the environment; for example, those who vote or work to protect ecosystems by setting aside habitats to save animals and resources; those who sell "dolphin-friendly tuna" and other environment-friendly products; and those who reduce their packaging and switch to recyclable packaging.

❏ Disagree with legislators, bureaucrats, businesses, and agencies who do not value the environment; for example, those who trade pollution credits rather than take initiative on cleaning air, water, and dump sites; those who waste or endanger resources such as fossil fuels, minerals, water, air, and forests.

❑ Write to the editorial page of local newspapers. Compliment, criticize, and comment on environmental issues, and encourage others to promote and create a fresh environmental philosophy. Have campers detail what they are doing environmentally at camp, too.

Note: Companies and governments use correspondence when determining how "the public"—their customers and voters—feel about a product or issue. The impact your campers can generate with 20 letters to a company or legislator equals that of a projected 120 to 220 consumers and/or voters.

According to the marketing departments of H.J. Heinz, Frito-Lay, A.C. Nielson, and Harris Poll, for every person who writes a compliment or protest letter, six to 11 more people feel the same way and don't. Rest assured, the companies your campers write to will respond, if only because adults don't want children to think they are "bad guys." Having children write also makes the activity newsworthy.

However, response time takes between six weeks and three months, so your campers will probably return home before the reply letters arrive. Add a standard cover letter of your own on camp letterhead, so corporations can send a response letter to you. Put any letters you receive in a clippings scrapbook to show to campers next season.

NEWSLETTERS PEOPLE KEEP

In this activity, campers will create a camp newsletter that informs friends and parents of their environmental accomplishments and build effective communication skills. Note: Be sure to print newsletter on both sides of the paper.

You'll need the following supplies:

❑ Pens/pencils and paper for reporters,
❑ Typewriter or computer,
❑ Printer,
❑ Mimeograph, ditto, or photocopy machine.

Organize a camp newsletter staff, appointing a counselor with a writing background as editor and campers as reporters and artists. Have camp reporters "cover" the camp environmental activities, and other activities. Remind them to interview those participating in programs, write the articles, and draw appropriate pictures. The articles can highlight projects they've completed, and give individuals' ideas for improving environmental efforts at home. Columns can be aimed at parents and siblings, explaining how to conserve resources. Campers can self-address and stamp the newsletters; you should mail them after the camp session.

You also may leave an empty page on the back for campers to write letters to themselves reminding them of ways they can help the Earth. Address the newsletter to the parents so they will read it. Mention to campers that they are conserving paper by sharing the letter with the newsletter.

OTHER ACTIVITIES

No matter which category of environmental awareness you choose to implement, you can offer campers these projects during arts and crafts sessions.

❏ Tie-dye or crayon batik cloth napkins that campers can use instead of the disposable paper napkins with their lunches.

❏ Offer art activities with water-based media (tempra, gouache, papier-mâché, glues, clays) and emphasize the basic relationship between art and water.

❏ Make colors and dyes from natural items. Create black from charcoal, red from strawberries, blue from black- and blueberries, yellow and brown from tomatoes, and green from grass.

❏ Create mobiles of animals and attach small representations of nature from their habitats.

❏ Make clay animal figures and create a base for them from scrap wood. Decorate the base with clay replicas of the animal's habitat or the vegetation it needs to survive.

❏ Create illustrations for the camp environmental newsletter.

❏ Make toy replicas of endangered species. Use a variety of materials and techniques (clay, wood, paper, origami, mobiles, models on stands). Have campers take them home or donate them to a day care in the community at the end of the session.

❏ Make posters presenting environmental issues, facts regarding endangered species, or information specific to the animals in your camp's ecosystem.

❏ Create a book about the camp environment covering topics such as environmental lessons campers studied, plans for a solar shower, or how to build a birdhouse. Make sure all campers who were involved in writing the book get a copy to take home, and donate a copy to the local library.

❏ When craft projects are completed, take pictures, and create space for public (or parental) viewing.

FINAL THOUGHTS

It's easy to develop activities to accompany your camp's environmental philosophy. Simply choose the categories you want to emphasize, and let your imagination roam free! If you find this creativity doesn't want to wander far, refer to the suggestions in this chapter, and then tailor the projects and questions to your age group.

The campers themselves often times provide the best ideas. By listening to their concerns, respecting their curiosity, and answering their questions through fun activities, you'll recruit an eager generation of people to join the environmental battle for our future.

3
INFRASTRUCTURE IMPROVEMENTS

4

HAZARDOUS AND TOXIC MATERIALS

"Life is simple until you add people."
—Bob Kalan, children's book author, Bellevue, Washington

One of the easiest ways to make friends with the environment is to adopt structural and operational practices that are kind to it. As the camp improves its site and physical plant, your participants will automatically use less energy and water and fewer hazardous materials and produce less waste. Making these physical changes generally requires only equipment and labor.

As you approach hazardous materials, however, certain ones can expose you to potentially costly liability. For example, if you find asbestos, pre-1979 fluorescent lighting containing PCBs, or a contaminated or empty underground tank, you must handle them promptly. You probably will want the help of a professional. Likewise, if your refrigerator(s), freezer(s) and/or air conditioner(s) run on CFC coolants such as freon, you must have them checked for leaks and, if necessary, repaired. You next should either retrofit them to use different coolants or replace them with new equipment. These and other items are covered in detail in this chapter.

To begin retrofitting your camp, you need to inventory the hazardous and toxic materials you have at camp and the scope of corrective actions you need to take. This season, if you haven't got urgent problems, such as asbestos or PCBs, you may decide simply to stop using hazardous materials for building maintenance. That's fine: You save your camp money for years to come, improve the septic or sewer systems (and consequently, your campers' health), and reduce your risk of liability. You also can use this type of situation to teach campers about the environment and about workplace safety. But don't stop there—tackle another area next year.

Limiting the scope of your project works to your advantage. Try too much, and your board, staff, and camp participants may resist, and end up discouraging everyone. Take small steps, and make them work, and everyone will have the confidence to continue.

WHAT ARE HAZARDOUS MATERIALS?

All "toxic" chemicals are hazardous, but not all "hazardous" chemicals are toxic. Ethanol (grain alcohol), for example, is hazardous, since it is flammable and will burn readily. In limited quantities, though, it can be ingested by humans and animals without causing illness or death. Ammonia, on the other hand, is toxic, but it is not a hazardous waste when you dispose of it. The industrial chemicals dioxin and PCB, creosote coating, and asbestos and the pesticide 2,4,5-T are both toxic and hazardous.

The simplest definitions of hazardous or toxic substances can be found on the labels of these products. Warnings may read:

❑ Caustic, corrosive, reactive,
❑ Ventilate area during use,
❑ Irritates skin and eyes,
❑ Wear protective clothing,
❑ Harmful or fatal if swallowed, and
❑ Keep out of reach of children.

Federal and state laws generally divide hazardous materials into two categories: extremely hazardous materials, which produce extremely hazardous wastes, and hazardous materials, which produce hazardous wastes. Obviously, the first category presents more danger to your camp than the second.

By federal and state regulations, hazardous materials are judged on four characteristics:

❑ Toxicity: in tiny doses, irreparably harmful or fatal to living things,
❑ Ignitability: a low flash point, or flammable at room temperature,
❑ Corrosivity: extremely acidic or alkaline; able to corrode steel, and
❑ Reactivity: unstable in air or water.

For complete definitions, listings, and laboratory testing criteria on hazardous materials, refer to the *Registry of Toxic Effects of Chemical Substances* (see Appendix A). Those lists are repeated and sometimes expanded in federal and state hazardous materials laws, and you can get additional information about the specific products you use by writing to the product manufacturer and asking for a Materials Safety Data Sheet (MSDS).

The Occupational Safety and Health Administration (OSHA) and some county regulations specify that Material Safety Data Sheets must be kept in a notebook or file whose location is known to all staff who handle such materials. You should also check local recommendations on training requirements, age restrictions, and handling and storage guidelines.

Hazardous materials are potential liabilities for any camp because they can cause harm far beyond their specific area of use. For example, if you dispose of antifreeze on the ground, animals are attracted to the sweet taste of the propylene glycol it contains and can kill themselves by lapping it up. If you use a pipe cleaner such as Drano® or Liquid Plumr® to clear a blockage, and your camp is on a septic system, you can destroy the bacteria that make the system work.

Environmental laws now place responsibility and liability for hazardous materials and their wastes at users' and manufacturers' doorsteps. The message is simple: whoever takes these substances into his or her possession is responsible for them until the substances and their containers are disposed of safely. If not disposed of safely, the user can be held liable indefinitely for that action, and for whatever damage is caused. There is no statute of limitations on hazardous waste damage.

The toxic and hazardous substances camps use most often are the same as those used in households. Hazardous waste laws define a household as one that turns out, every month, 1 kilogram (2.2 pounds) or less of extremely hazardous waste; or spill-cleanup debris containing extremely hazardous waste, and/or 100 kilograms (220 pounds) or less of hazardous waste; or spill-cleanup debris containing hazardous waste. Entities turning out more than these quantities are called "large-quantity generators."

More and more localities across North America now stage weekend household hazardous waste roundups as an alternative for people who would otherwise throw out toxics with their garbage. Most localities collect over 200 different types of toxic materials that fall into the following categories:

❑ Paints, inks, dyes, and coatings (spray, oil-based, latex);

❑ Pesticides, fungicides, and herbicides;

❑ Antifreeze, waste motor oil, and other automotive fluids;

❑ Solvents, flushes, and degreasers;

❑ Aerosols;

❑ Adhesives, cements, and glazes;

❑ Corrosives (acids and bases);

❑ Pharmaceuticals and cosmetics;

❑ Photo chemicals;

❑ Mercury, PCB ballasts, and heavy metals;

❑ Batteries (wet cell and dry cell);

❑ Smoke alarms;

❑ Gas cylinders;

❑ Cleaning agents.

Latex paints are water soluble and not considered hazardous. Small quantities can be flushed down sanitary sewers. But during roundups, localities often host latex paint swaps, where the public can exchange specific colors, or the organizers mix similar colors and offer them free of charge. (This is a good place for camps to get free paint.) Oil-based paints are hazardous, and must be disposed of properly.

GETTING ANSWERS ABOUT TOXIC AND HAZARDOUS MATERIALS

Local, state, and federal hazardous materials laws can affect your operations, real estate transactions, and the materials you use and handle on site. But the laws on hazardous materials not only differ from city to city across America, they constantly evolve, too. Thus, it's recommended you stay aware of current legal developments in order to continue in compliance.

Different authorities at the federal, state, and local levels handle different areas of law, so you may have to make more than one phone call to get answers. The good news is most agencies have printed materials they can send you, and some have libraries to aid your research. The following agencies can assist you on each level:

❏ Federal: call or write your regional Environmental Protection Agency (EPA) office or OSHA office.

❏ State: call the local, regional, or state capital office of your state's department of ecology, environment, public works, natural resources, or OSHA.

❏ Local: call your municipal or county solid waste management or environment department.

❏ General questions: call any of the preceding agencies first. If you don't get an answer (which is very unlikely), call the environmental writer at your local newspaper, or check the *Yellow Pages* under "Consultants—Environmental," "Consultants—Engineering," "Engineers—Environmental," "Conservation and Ecological Organizations," or "Environmental and Ecological Services."

HAZARDOUS MATERIALS HANDLING AND DISPOSAL

Jurisdictions in most North American states and provinces now suggest the following guidelines for handling hazardous materials:

❏ Source reduction: use less hazardous or toxic materials to do a job, and substitute safe materials for toxic ones.

❏ Reuse: for example, filter paint thinner for use again.

❏ Recycle: for example, explore lubricating camp vehicle engines with recycled oil.

❏ Proper disposal: preferably use a hazardous-waste collection event. Call your local solid waste management division for information and upcoming dates.

Many jurisdictions require you to dispose of hazardous wastes separately from your regular garbage; if yours doesn't it soon may since this is the trend. Some general rules to follow:

❏ Buy only as much hazardous material as you need, and use it all before buying more.

❏ If you buy an aerosol can, turn it upside down after it's empty, and then press the nozzle to let out all the propellant before disposing of the can.

❏ Start a hazardous materials inventory plan. Document whatever hazardous materials you buy, and prepare a check-out sheet for those items. Ask your staff to sign out and in these materials as they use them. Refer to Worksheet 4–1 at the end of this chapter for a guide.

❏ Set aside a separate trash container for hazardous wastes, and contact your trash hauler or solid waste department to learn the appropriate way to transport the container to a certified hazardous materials dump.

❏ Wrap leaking or otherwise contaminated objects in watertight plastic bags before disposing of them properly.

❏ Filter paint thinners and other solvents for re-use, and store in airtight containers (read product directions to know if they should be kept in a cool place).

❏ If you do your own mechanical and maintenance work, equip your mechanic and groundspeople with the necessary equipment and containers for handling hazardous materials such as motor and machine lubricants, fuels, and coolants. Also, learn where you can recycle these and other items such as car batteries, and appliances such as refrigerators and freezers. The easiest way to handle vehicle wastes is to simply get the work done at a garage.

❏ Whenever you, your staff, or contractors work with hazardous materials, document it. Make certain your contractors are licensed and bonded. Check their references and documents before they start work.

❏ Make sure your staff are trained in the proper use, handling, and disposal of any hazardous materials they use.

COMMON HAZARDOUS MATERIALS

There are thousands of hazardous materials now on the market, but only about 200 are available to the public—the rest are used by industry. Your camp should first concentrate on eliminating banned items: the coatings penta and creosote and the pesticides DDT, chlorodane, 2,4,5–T, and silvex. If you don't have these specific products, read ingredients labels. You may find them included in gardening, maintenance, and home-care products.

Most furniture polishes and many spot removers contain mineral spirits and petroleum distillates such as terpene hydrocarbons. Some spray shoe polishes contain perchlorethylene. Nail polish is the same as oil-based enamel paint, and polish remover is acetone. Many detergents contain caustics and arsenic.

Now that you have a clearer idea of which materials are toxic and hazardous materials, consider substituting safer products wherever you can. For specific guidance, keep a *Household Hazardous Waste Wheel* from the Environmental Hazards Management Institute on site (see Appendix A). Meanwhile, use up the stock you have, and then call your waste management company, county cooperative extension agent, or municipal or county solid waste department for advice on how best to dispose of it.

HIGHLY PUBLICIZED TOXICS

Here is a short explanation of the more publicized toxic items, and where you might find them present at your camp. Many of these items will be banned from use this decade; new regulations are being considered on the others.

PCBs: oily dielectric fluids used to insulate distribution transformers, as a ballast for fluorescent light fixtures, and in some carbonless copy papers. PCBs are carcinogenic, accumulate in animal fat, and remain stable in the environment for decades. Banned after 1979.

CFCs: widely used in coolant liquids for refrigerators, freezers, and air conditioners; in propellants for aerosol toys and party, boat, and sports horns; and in cleaners for circuit boards and office equipment. CFCs are harmful to the Earth's ozone layer because, once released, they rise into the high atmosphere where ultraviolet light bombardment breaks them apart, releasing their chlorine molecules to combine with free oxygen atoms in the ozone. Due to be banned as of December 31, 1995.

Halons: CFC relatives that contain bromine, chlorine, or fluorine. They are used in fire suppressant systems for airplanes, moisture-sensitive environments such as computer rooms, and in fire extinguishers; and are more harmful to the ozone layer than CFCs. Due to be banned December 31, 1995.

Methyl chloroform: a CFC relative used as an active ingredient in aerosol degreasers and solvents, adhesives, coatings, inks, vapor degreasing for metals and electronics, and manufacturing fluorocarbons. It, too, is harmful to the ozone. Due to be banned December 31, 1995.

Carbon tetrachloride: This toxic is a carcinogenic and ozone-harmful compound used in the production of pesticides, fluorocarbons, pharmaceuticals, and other chemicals. It is due to be banned in December of 1995.

Formaldehyde: used as an ingredient in carpeting, foamed-in-place structural wall insulation, particle-board adhesives, and other products, and released from them as a toxic gas. Many people appear to be adversely affected by this gas, and medical agencies are now collecting and assessing allergy data. The results may lead to restrictions on the use of this chemical and re-formulation of products in which it is used.

Radon: an odorless, colorless, tasteless radioactive gas formed from decaying uranium. Radon's half-life is only a matter of days. It percolates from the ground in North America where uranium and radon are found in trace amounts in most soils and rocks. Dry, porous, and permeable soils, and fractured or faulted rock allow this gas through easily; wet, tight clay soils don't. Granite, shale, and phosphate contain more radon than dark volcanic rock.

Radon is a concern because researchers have discovered it can accumulate inside closed spaces such as homes and buildings. There, static charges attach it to dust and vapor. Humans inhale it and expose their lung tissue to small bursts of radiated energy as the radon continues to decay. This can eventually generate cancer growth.

The risk of radon cancer at camps is small, unless the gas is contained in a closed space and you're exposed to it daily over a long period of weeks. Otherwise, radon simply mixes with the outdoor air and usually is too diluted to be harmful.

Lead-acid car batteries: all states now ban these from disposal in landfills and require that they be recycled at certified facilities. In many states, people who buy new batteries pay a small "core charge" or "advance diversion fee" at purchase to help cover the cost of recycling the battery when it is finished.

EVERYDAY TOXICS

The toxic substance list, unfortunately, includes far more than highly publicized chemicals. A host of everyday items also create environmental damage. Here are some of the most recognizable:

Fuels, including gasoline, diesel, white gas, methane, propane, natural gas, lighter fluid, and charcoal briquette fluid. All evaporate at room temperature, giving off fumes that are flammable and harmful when inhaled.

Lubricants and fluids—for vehicles and machinery—that are all harmful or fatal if swallowed, and can irritate skin. Animals particularly love the sweet taste of the propylene glycol in antifreeze, and lap it up where it spills on the ground. This usually kills them.

Pesticides, used for killing insects; the liquids and vapors are harmful or fatal to humans and animals.

Herbicides, used for killing plants; the liquids and vapors are harmful or fatal to humans and animals.

Dishwashing detergents that contain phosphates and arsenic. The phosphates contribute to cancerous algae growth that chokes the fish in lakes and streams. The arsenic is a heavy metal that helps render sewage sludge unusable as fertilizer.

Oil-based and metallic paints, including inks, dyes, and coatings, and the mineral spirits, thinners, solvents, and degreasers used to thin and clean them. All give off fumes that are harmful to humans and animals.

Infectious and other medical wastes, including used bandages, blood and other bodily fluids, pharmaceuticals, and sharps (blades and needles). (Note: OSHA requires a documented Exposure Control Plan for providing health care and dealing with medical waste. The American Camping Association accreditation standards highly recommend this plan as well to minimize exposure to health hazards. This plan must include "universal precautions" for dealing with blood and bodily fluids.)

SOLUTIONS TO HANDLING HAZARDOUS AND TOXIC MATERIALS

The best way to handle hazardous and toxic materials is not to buy them. But if you must buy them, get the smallest amount you need for the job, and use the entire amount.

To handle these materials, use recommended protective clothing, such as heavy-duty neoprene or other industrial-grade gloves, goggles, masks, overalls, and boots as necessary. Don't use latex dish-washing gloves; solvents dissolve them. You can find appropriate gloves and other protective clothing at building supply, hardware, and safety-supply stores.

Here are specific steps to protect yourself when handling specific materials:

Penta, creosote, DDT, chlordane, 2,4,5–T, silvex: If you find these items at your camp, contact your municipal or county solid waste management authority, or state ecology or environment department for procedures on how to handle, use, and dispose of them.

PCBs: Less than 50 parts per million is considered a safe level for this toxic. Your local electric company most likely has addressed its transformers at your camp, and you probably are not using 1979 carbonless forms. However, the ballast in your fluorescent light fixtures may be another matter.

Depending on the manufacturer, the ballast may be located at one end, and run the length of the fixture openly, or it may be tucked inside the fixture. If the ballast is not apparent, find the manufacturer's brand, call an electrical supply house, and ask where it is on that fixture. The ballast should either have a date or a "No PCB" stamp.

If you find a tar-like substance on the fixture, it may be from the PCB ballasts, which can break down after 10 to 15 years. Don't worry. First, check the floor underneath the fixture for drips. Open a window, or otherwise ventilate the area. If the floor is a hard surface, wipe up the drips with a paper towel; if carpet, cut out the stained patch. Get *two* plastic garbage bags, and place one inside the other. Remove the fixture and wrap it with the dirty towel or carpet in the double bag, then call your disposal company or local solid waste department to ask how best to dispose of it. As of 1992, federal law allows people to dispose of up to four fixtures in their regular garbage pickup, but that may change as hazardous waste disposal becomes more convenient for the public, and laws focus more directly on household hazardous wastes.

CFCs: These fall mostly within the scope of the air conditioning and refrigeration industries, which are specifically regulated by federal and other statutes. However, CFCs have been and still are used in some styrofoam products. The compound replacing most CFCs in foam containers is HCFC, which has one tenth the harmful punch of CFC but is still due to be banned in the year 2030.

Still, you should (1) avoid buying disposable styrofoam products, unless no other item fits the purpose, (2) recycle the styrofoam you do buy, and (3) any time your refrigeration units are serviced, make certain the technician is certified and uses certified recapture equipment to recycle the refrigerant. Check and record the technician's license number and credentials, the action he or she takes, and the date of each service call. By law, no CFCs can be released or "vented" into the atmosphere during servicing.

When you decide to replace your old refrigerator, freezer, car air conditioner, or indoor air conditioner, call your local solid waste management division to learn about disposal options. For a small fee, appliance stores, car dealerships, and other businesses will take the unit, capture the freon, and handle the disposal of it.

Halons: If you have a halon fire extinguisher, the EPA suggests that you not worry about causing environmental harm with it. When the life-span expires, dispose of it as hazardous waste, and replace it with new equipment which does not contain the material.

Methyl chloroform: Used in degreasing solvents, it is aromatic and must be used in ventilated areas. Handle with rubber gloves and protective clothing, store in a sealed container, and dispose of it as a hazardous waste.

Carbon tetrachloride: This toxic is a carcinogenic and ozone-harmful compound used in the production of pesticides, fluorocarbons, pharmaceuticals, and other chemicals. It is virtually unavailable for anything other than industrial applications and is due to be banned in December of 1995. If you find it packaged as a product, or included in the ingredients list of any products you have on site, dispose of it as a hazardous waste.

Radon: As noted earlier, the risk of radon poisoning is small, unless the gas becomes contained in a closed space where people spend a lot of time. Generally, the only spaces that qualify at camp are offices. If you use the offices year-round, there may be some concern if you find high levels of the gas. If the spaces are always ventilated, or used only in seasons when you keep the windows open, you'll also have little to worry about.

Radon gas seeps into buildings mostly through cracks in cinderblock and foundation floors. It also can enter around loose-fitting drainage pipes; through sump pumps, tap water, and building materials; and between the building foundation and surrounding soil because of pressure differentials.

Researchers still don't understand radon's migration patterns. Building construction and soil characteristics are factors, but radon concentrations can vary enormously among neighboring buildings over similar soil, or among seemingly identical buildings.

So the first step in radon control is to test your buildings with a radon detector. These generally are available for approximately $20 through hardware, grocery, and other retail outlets. If you can't find them there, call your regional EPA office for a referral.

According to the EPA, less than four picocuries per liter (4 pCi/L) is not considered a harmful level; 4 to 20 pCi/L indicates a need to correct the situation within a year; a 20 to 200 pCi/L level means correct the situation within a few months; more than 200 pCi/L means attend to the problem within weeks. If this isn't feasible, increase ventilation to the space or relocate temporarily until the problem is resolved.

Each building is unique, so a radon reduction technique that works in one may not work in another. If you find high levels in one or more of your structures, it's wise to conduct an inspection to pinpoint radon sources and make your reduction program more effective. Again, your regional EPA office will be able to give you inspection directions, or look under "Radon Testing" in the *Yellow Pages.*

After you isolate the radon's sources, use one or all of the following ways to cut those high levels. In each case, make sure your choice becomes a permanent part of your building's operations (for specific information, see Appendix A).

❏ House ventilation: This is a temporary solution; basically, open windows and doors. This works in good weather but not in bad, and not over the long term. Use it only until you set up a permanent solution.

❏ Soil-gas suction and pressure control: The first reduces air pressure under the foundation to a level less than that in the house, drawing away the radon into the air vents. The second increases pressure under the foundation to a level greater than that in the soil, keeping the radon from entering the building substructure.

❏ Sealing: Seal cracks in foundation and around plumbing and electrical openings in walls and foundations to prevent the radon's entry. If the gas is still present after using this method, refer to soil-gas suction and pressure control.

Fuels: Keep tanks and containers sealed unless they are in use, and then use in well-ventilated areas, taking care not to spill. Most fuel will be handled by authorized personnel, such as your oil- or gas-company driver or representative. If you are pumping gas for vehicles on site, equip your pump nozzle with a collar that prevents fumes from escaping into the air when you fill. Report any large (5 gallons or more) fuel spill immediately to your EPA or Coast Guard hazardous materials hotline, or to your fire department or local hazardous materials authority.

Avoid using lighter fluid to light charcoal briquettes. It burns dirty like diesel fuel and can be spilled easily. Instead, start the fire with paper in a metal or tinfoil charcoal chimney under the charcoal. Or use an electric starter, a gas grill, or charcoal fire-starting gel, paraffin sticks, or treated wood chips.

Make sure that all staff using stoves or lanterns have been trained in the proper use of the particular equipment and the proper handling of the fuel. (Stove and lantern fuels include propane, butane, kerosene, white gas, and alcohol.) To minimize risk while using a lantern or stove, always read any manufacturer's instructions before use. Also follow these general guidelines: Keep activity around the cook site to a minimum, place the stove or lantern on a level surface, make certain the fuel canister is seated correctly to avoid leakage, never allow anyone to have his or her face near a stove or lantern when it is being lighted, and never remove a fuel canister while a stove or lantern is running.

Caustics, corrosives, and reactives: Avoid using these if possible. If not, purchase only as much as you plan to use, and use the entire amount in a well-ventilated area, protecting yourself with industrial-grade neoprene gloves and other appropriate clothing (face mask, safety glasses, boots) if necessary. Follow the manufacturer's instructions. Dispose of the excess, or the empty container, as hazardous waste. Report any spill immediately to your EPA or Coast Guard hazardous materials hotline, or fire department or local hazardous materials authority.

Never pour the substances down the drain, on a gravel or paved road, in a stream, or even on ground where you want to kill weeds anyway. They damage sewage treatment systems and ruin sludge for use as fertilizer; pollute ground water; and kill plants, insects, and animals indiscriminately.

Vehicle and machinery lubricants, fluids, and degreasers: These are necessary to run the machinery on which our lives depend. The main concern is not to spill them. Store them in sealed containers, use in ventilated areas, and dispose of them properly. Most lubricants can be recycled, and your municipal or county solid waste management department can direct you to recyclers.

Never pour these substances down the drain, on a gravel or paved road, in a stream, or even on ground where you want to kill weeds anyway. They damage sewage treatment systems and ruin sludge for use as fertilizer; pollute ground water; and kill plants, insects, and animals indiscriminately.

Pesticides/Insecticides: Don't use these unnecessarily. They are dangerous, mutagenic (DNA/gene-altering) poisons. Most insect problems can be solved by other means. For example, you can remove or seal up food and other items that attract them; find and fill holes they use to enter buildings; put screens on doors and windows; remove their nests from buildings and activity areas; introduce insect predators such as ladybugs and preying mantises. For slugs in the garden, plant sacrificial flora such as marigolds, repellent buds of garlic and onion, and, as a last resort, use poison pellets. Borax and citrus-based products also work well against insect pests. For more advice, call the National Coalition Against the Misuse of Pesticides, at 202-543-5450.

Pesticides should only be used as a last resort in cases where carpenter ants or termites infest your building's structure, for example, or predatory, debilitating insects infest your garden or orchard. Use products that have short lives (ask nursery personnel or agricultural extension agents for advice). Handle all pesticides with gloves and protective clothing, store in sealed containers, and dispose of them as hazardous waste.

Never pour pesticides down the drain, on a gravel or paved road, in a stream, or even on ground where you want to kill weeds anyway. They damage sewage treatment systems and ruin sludge for use as fertilizer; pollute ground water; and kill plants, insects, and animals indiscriminately.

Herbicides: Don't use these unnecessarily; they are dangerous, mutagenic poisons. Most weed and plant problems can be solved by other means. Dig them out, rototill them under, or prune or chop back fast-growing plants. As a last resort, in the case of blackberry and other invasive vine plants with deep and virtually uncontrollable root systems for example, chop them back to the roots, then brush a small amount of a fast-decaying weed killer full strength, on the end of the exposed root. Again, ask nursery personnel or agricultural extension agents for advice on poisons that break down into harmless substances within a few days or weeks. This method is slower than spraying herbicide; still, it minimizes your use of poison.

Between uses, handle all herbicides with protective clothing, store in sealed containers, and dispose of as hazardous waste. *Never* pour herbicide down the drain, on a gravel or paved road, in a stream, or even on ground where you want to kill weeds anyway. They damage sewage treatment systems and ruin sludge for use as fertilizer; pollute ground water; and kill plants, insects, and animals indiscriminately.

Warning: No pesticide, herbicide, or insecticide label explains the content's potency against each type of flora, nor how frequently to apply or re-apply it. Rather, there is usually a list of plants against which it is effective, and general mixing instructions for the necessary quantities. Thus, people routinely overuse these poisons, fouling living areas and contaminating plants, animals, utensils, foods, and water supplies.

The worst offenders tend to be farmers trying to protect their crops from insects and weeds. Farmers around the world routinely overuse herbicides, which are borne off by rainwater to contaminate lakes, streams, and ground water.

At the very least, keep records of when and where you use these chemicals to avoid over-application and consequent contamination.

Oil-based and metallic paints, (including dyes, inks, solvents, and coatings): Avoid using these if possible. If not, purchase only as much as you plan to use, use the entire amount in a well-ventilated area, and dispose of it as a hazardous waste.

Solvents and thinners (mineral spirits) can often be reused by filtering them through paper coffee filters, doubled cheesecloth, or other fine mesh screens. *Never* pour them down the drain, on a gravel or paved road, in a stream, or even on ground where you want to kill weeds anyway. They damage sewage treatment systems and ruin sludge for use as fertilizer; pollute ground water; and kill plants, insects, and animals indiscriminately.

Whenever possible, substitute water-based products for oil- and lead-based materials. For example, latex enamels can be thinned with water, shellac can be thinned with alcohol, and woods can be finished with linseed oil, lemon oil, and beeswax. Also, learn how to make dyes and tints from local forest and farm products (e.g., red from strawberries, yellow/orange from tomatoes, brown from bark), and how to get clay from local earth.

Infectious and other medical wastes: Most jurisdictions permit you to flush out-of-date pharmaceuticals and bodily fluids down the sanitary sewers. Sharps must be sealed in an impervious container, such as a plastic soda or milk jug, and the cap taped closed.

In general, routine sanitary procedures for disposing small amounts of medical waste are sufficient. Disposable towels and tissues or bandages contaminated with blood should be placed in a trash container lined with plastic. Tied plastic bags can then be put in the regular trash for disposal.

Persons involved in cleaning contaminated surfaces should avoid exposing open skin lesions or mucous membranes to blood or bodily fluids. Whenever possible, use disposable towels or tissues, and then properly discard them. Mops should be rinsed in disinfectant.

Regulated medical waste (i.e., liquid or semi-liquid blood, or items with blood on them) should be placed in closable and labeled or color-coded containers for proper disposal.

Call your local health department for additional guidelines.

Dishwashing and other detergents: Ask your supplier about the ingredients in your detergent, and find substitutes if you are using products that contain phosphates and/or arsenic. Though they may irritate skin, no special protective clothing is required when handling them. Among the new products to try are dish detergents from companies such as Mountain Fresh Products, Bi-O-Kleen, and Life Tree.

Household degreasers, solvents, and cleaners: Handle these with gloves, and substitute white vinegar, baking soda, and even Coca Cola® with a little "elbow grease" to clean most surfaces. Coke is great for chrome. There are a number of more powerful environmentally friendly products available, too, such as Clean Green and citrus-based cleaners.

For quick-reference advice on hazardous materials, get a "Household Hazardous Waste Wheel" (see Appendix A).

Insurers have become very sticky about high-liability items such as hazardous materials and wastes on their clients' properties. This is because they have been stung for billions of dump cleanup and health-related lawsuit dollars in the past decade alone. As your first course of action, discuss this matter with your insurer to learn what coverage your policy provides, and whether you need to take any action.

If you have any concerns about your property, you may wish to inventory hazardous materials, underground tanks, and potential dump areas. If you discover anything amiss, take immediate remedial action. If you handle hazardous materials at camp, set up an inventory system in which you purchase only what you need, and allow only those who have been trained in proper use and disposal to sign out the materials. Finally, if you plan to purchase another property, have it completely audited by a licensed and bonded hazardous materials specialist prior to entering into any purchasing negotiations.

THE BIG A: ASBESTOS

You may already have encountered warnings and publicity about asbestos. Nevertheless, some background information is in order.

Asbestos was used prior to 1977 for four main purposes:

1. to strengthen product material;
2. as electrical and thermal insulation in appliances, buildings, heating and cooling systems, and thermal clothing;
3. for acoustical insulation and interior decoration;
4. for fire protection.

Unfortunately, before people discovered how dangerous it is, asbestos was used in a wide variety of products: pre-1977 hair dryers, stoves and slow cookers, ceiling and floor tiles, sprayed-on ceiling coatings, wall and pipe coverings, roofing and siding materials, brake and clutch linings, insulation in houses built or remodeled between 1930 and 1950, and many more.

There is no safe level of asbestos for humans to ingest. However, it doesn't pose a health problem unless it is released as fibrous, microscopic dust into the air people breathe.

So, unless it is crumbling, or *friable* as the trade calls it, the EPA and state authorities say asbestos doesn't need repair or removal. To be certain, check your camp for the following conditions:

❏ Is the asbestos sealed by some form of coating—either an adhesive sealant tape or a penetrating or bridging *encapsulant* (paint or other coating)? This applies to items such as "popcorn" ceilings, water or furnace pipe insulation jackets, and outdoor siding products.

❏ Is the asbestos in a *nonfriable* form, such as floor tile, roofing materials, packing, or gaskets?

If you have any questions, call your local air pollution control authority, department of public health, EPA, or an asbestos contractor (in the *Yellow Pages* under "Asbestos," or "Waste Disposal—Hazardous") to inspect the situation. They will advise you on its condition and the action to take, and will handle sealing or removal if that's necessary. If the asbestos is in good repair, however, it is harmless as long as it remains encapsulated.

Given the danger posed by asbestos dust in the air, it isn't a good idea to attempt sealant or removal work yourself. Removal work is very expensive, due to the intricate handling procedures required by law, so your most economical alternative—if it's an option for you—is to leave the asbestos in place and have it sealed. If the asbestos you encounter *is* in a friable form, such as in personal heating appliances, hair dryers, and slow cookers manufactured before 1977, wrap it carefully (as carefully as if you were sneaking up on a wasp nest) in a heavy plastic bag, and call for advice on disposing of it.

If you plan to upgrade your central heating or water heating system and it has asbestos-jacketed pipes, you'll need to contact a licensed asbestos removal contractor to handle that part of refitting your system (see Chapter 5 for more information). Take the same action if any of your remodeling projects involve handling asbestos.

If you do any of this work yourself, you may be held liable for the next 30 years for any health problems people can trace back to contact with your work. Don't risk it. Your local authorities can advise you on the proper action, and point you toward contractors.

If you go with a contractor, make certain he or she is bonded, licensed, and certified by the state to perform this job. Check references, and record the contractor's name, license number, the dates he or she performs the work, and the disposal action taken. Asbestos is a hazardous waste that cannot be dumped in household garbage, at a transfer station, or in dumpsters. It must go only to a hazardous waste dump.

If you must clean up a space where you've found asbestos debris, wear a head mask, gloves, and protective clothing; put the debris into a clearly marked, thick plastic bag; then mop up the dust with wet rags and drop them in the bag, too.

THE BIG U: UNDERGROUND TANKS

Underground tanks can be camps' second biggest concern if leakage contaminates soil and groundwater, exposing the camp to fines and lawsuits. Under federal and state laws, the owner of any property where a tank is buried is liable for any damage the tank or its contents do.

Most underground fuel tanks have 15- to 30-year lifetimes. Some give out sooner, some later, depending on the moisture and acidity in the tank's contents and its surrounding soil. In either case, when the tanks begin to corrode, they can leak their toxic liquids into the ground, and hence into the ground water.

If you have tanks on camp property, you are responsible for investigating which agency and which codes govern your locality. Depending on where you are, the buried tank enforcement authority will either be the local fire department, the department of environment, ecology, hazardous materials or solid waste management in your county, municipality, or state.

If you have one or more unused tanks on your property, the local code may require you to (1) dig down and remove them, or, if you leave them in the ground, (2) cleanse and fill them with liquid concrete or other slurry or cured polyurethane. However, there are drawbacks to using either of these fillers. If the tank is filled with slurry, and ultimately must be removed, it will be much heavier and harder to handle than it was empty. If your area has a high water table, the polyurethane may provide all the buoyancy the tank needs to start floating up through the ground.

If you must remove a tank, call your oil company for advice, or check the *Yellow Pages* under "Oils—Waste," "Tanks—Removal," "Waste Disposal," or "Environmental Services." Professional removal can cost up to $2,000. No matter who removes the tank, document the action and keep the records accessible.

FINAL THOUGHTS

Because of the immediate and long-term damage hazardous and toxic materials can inflict on their surroundings, handling them is serious business. Your best course of action is to avoid them, if possible. Beyond that, follow all instructions, wear proper protective clothing, and always check with the appropriate authorities for advice on disposal. Your camp will be safer both from a health and a legal standpoint.

WORKSHEET 4-1
HAZARDOUS MATERIALS CHECKOUT

STORAGE LOCATION _____

HAZARDOUS MATERIAL	CHECKOUT					CHECKIN		
	DATE	USE	VOLUME	NAME OF USER	THIS PERSON HAS BEEN TRAINED IN THE USE OF MATERIAL	DATE	VOLUME	RESEALED

5
WATER CONSERVATION

"Waste not, want not."
—European folk saying

Programming Idea

Over time, you may be surprised to see campers bring new water-saving habits with them to camp. These may include shutting off the shower while soaping, turning off the water between rinses while brushing their teeth, washing a car with a bucket of water rather than with a hose; and cleaning walks and streets with a push broom rather than using a hose. If participants don't bring these habits from home, suggest they practice them at camp to see how well they work.

Scientists say there are nearly 386,000,000,000,000 (386 trillion) gallons of water on Earth at any given time. But, in one year, the average American uses 5,000 gallons of water just to take showers. The average 25–yard swimming pool, depending on its bottom design, holds between 150,000 and 185,000 gallons. So although trillions of gallons seems like an inexhaustible amount, the truth is there's not enough to meet the world's demands. Everyone needs to be more conscious of water use—including your staff and campers.

There are two key conservation methods that work best in any environmental program:

1. Don't use it.
2. Use less.

A good way to begin applying those principles at your camp is to install equipment that demands fewer resources (e.g., low-flow shower heads). Your second step is to regulate water use.

Installing more efficient equipment during the off-season is often easier than trying to change people's usage habits in-season. But if you encourage campers to invest in the changes by getting them involved in activities such as measuring usage and installing new plumbing, the conservation cooperation will improve. Either way, your action(s) will save camp operating costs from this season on by reducing your camp's water demands.

A Closer Look

Understand your water company statement. In most areas of the country, water is charged per 100 cubic feet (748 gallons) used. This amount of water is also called a unit. From these statements, determine how much water your facility uses each month and each season.

This chapter provides an overview of water conservation measures you can implement. First, contact your local water company for conservation information, rebate and loan programs, and referrals to consulting and equipment companies. If there is conservation equipment on the market that you can't obtain from a local supplier, refer to the catalog houses in Appendix A.

Now, calculate the flow rates of your faucets and shower heads. You can do the simple arithmetic yourself. Simply set a 1-or 5-gallon bucket under a tap or shower head, turn on the water full blast, and with a watch, time how long it takes to fill the bucket. If it takes 30 seconds to fill a 5-gallon bucket, your flow rate per minute is (5 gallons/30 seconds) × (60 seconds/1 minute), or 10 gallons/minute. If possible, perform those calculations with both your current equipment and samples of the new water conservation items so you can accurately compare costs on the worksheets at the end of this chapter.

There are two purposes for these calculations:

1. to learn where you use your water and how much you use in each place, and

2. to learn how many gallons and dollars you will save by implementing your conservation program.

Finally, follow the step-by-step suggestions and worksheets in this chapter. They will help you determine which actions are feasible and which are not, what equipment is necessary, and what your camp's costs will be. When completed, the worksheets are handy tools for presenting your dramatic gains to your camp board, campers, and staff.

TOILET TANK WATER USAGE

Programming Idea

Whenever possible:

❏ *Have campers calculate the water usage,*

❏ *Create a reward system for accomplishing a conservation goal. It doesn't have to be involved; a certificate, a watermelon, or a bedtime guitar performance by a favorite counselor for the cabin group is sufficient.*

Tank toilets that need more than four gallons of water to flush consume nearly 25 percent of a household's (and a camp's) water usage each day. Reducing the number of flushes reduces the amount of water used. Though not acceptable to all, you might begin with this simplest of water-saving ideas: "If it's yellow, let it mellow; if it's brown, flush it down" (anonymous).

Or, you can reduce the amount of water your toilets use per flush by inserting water displacers or dams in the tanks, or by installing low-gallonage flush units. The first is the less expensive of these two options, but it should be only an interim step because it reduces flush water by a gallon a time at most. While more expensive, new equipment can cut usage in half, by 3 to 6 gallons per flush. Therefore, if your municipal government or water company will pay you a subsidy, it may be worth replacing your large-tank toilets with either 1.5- or 3-gallon tank-style units or institutional-style air flush units.

If you wish to avoid the expense of new equipment, try the quicker and more enjoyable option of organizing campers and staff to put displacers or dams in your current tank toilets.

Your operations or programming staff can use the following instructions to install toilet tank displacers (see Figure 5-1):

Potential Pitfall

Some people complain that a 1.5-gallon unit doesn't provide enough water to do a complete flushing job, and must be flushed twice. Solicit you local water department's, plumbing supplier's, or bath showroom's advice on specific brands that avoid this situation. Also refer to Consumer Reports, *which periodically compares different toilet brands.*

1. Save empty 1-liter and 2-liter clear plastic (PET) soda bottles.
2. See which bottle sizes fit in tank toilets.
3. Weight each with a few stones, fill with water, and recap.
4. Anchor one bottle by its neck to the inside of each toilet tank with nylon fishing line and drapery hooks or stiff wire.

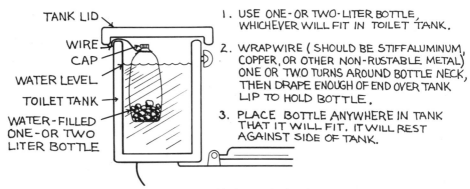

Figure 5-1. Toilet tank displacer

A gray water system, which recirculates sink and shower water for toilets, outdoor watering, and other purposes that don't require drinking-quality water, is an expensive option, but one worth considering if subsidies or loans are available. Investigate codes and feasibility and permit requirements with your health department and water utility. Talk with a plumbing contractor about installation. Remember that only biodegradable soaps and toiletries can be used in such a system.

Refer to Worksheet 5-1: Toilet Tank Displacers at the end of this chapter to calculate your camp's potential dollar savings.

SHOWER HEAD WATER USAGE

A Closer Look

Putting displacers in toilet tanks saves a quart to a half-gallon of water every time someone flushes a camp toilet.

Low-flow shower head units with shut-off buttons can cut your shower water usage by up to half, or 10 to 15 gallons per shower per person. However, it costs more initially to replace shower heads than to set displacers in toilet tanks. If you compare initial costs to long-term dollar savings, you will be prepared to justify the shower head cost to your board, owner, or accountant. (See Worksheet 5-2: Shower Head Water Waste at the end of this chapter to help you calculate those amounts for your camp.)

After completing Worksheet 5-2, fill out Worksheet 5-3: Water Use Action List to organize your shower head replacement project.

LAWN AND GARDEN WATER USAGE

Outdoors, water generally is used for plants and lawns; hosing sidewalks, drives, and playing areas; and at drinking fountains. You can control the water waste for each of these usages without much expense.

Nearly half the water usage at an average camp each season is devoted to keeping plants and lawns alive. To reduce your camp's water usage in this category, first ask yourself if your plants are the right ones for your environment. Trying to grow plants outside their climate zones generally begs for problems: pests, diseases, and additional water and labor. You don't see cherry trees in a desert, nor do you see saguaro cactus in the Northwest. To xeriscape properly, examine your climate zone, contact your county cooperative extension agent or local nursery, and design a mix of trees and plants appropriate to your biome and ecosystem.

When you plant, do it in early spring while the ground is still wet, or in the fall as everything goes dormant. Don't plant in hot weather; you'll need heavier amounts of water to anchor the turf, shrub, or tree into the ground. In fact, if your plantings are climate-compatible (with the exception of many annuals), they shouldn't need much additional water in the hot season because they have evolved to survive in their ecosystem's seasons.

Other keys to healthy low-water lawns and gardens:

❏ Arrange plants, trees, etc., to cover or shade the ground you water and to slow evaporation from the ground. Blanket tree bases with mulch to hold moisture and surrender as little water as possible to evaporation. Water the trees between the outside of the mulch line and the drip line—the outermost area of ground where branches hang.

   Some trees may be harmed by having mulch around their bases, because it can harbor parasites that damage the crop. Ask your local plant nursery for advice.

❏ Don't water the tree base, unless it is a new planting and you want to keep the root ball moist.

Next, practice grass-cycling: cut your grass 1 1/2 to 2 inches high, and let the clippings settle in among the live stalks and die as mulch. If you would rather rake it, you can use this as green material for composting rather than send it to a landfill (see Chapter 7 for additional information).

You also can use these grass clippings to conserve water (and control weeds) by placing them as mulch around plants. (Compost; chipped wood limbs, branches, and bark; commercial mulch; and leaves make good mulch too.)

When forming your camp's approach to lawns, note that grass and trees are not necessarily compatible. Grass needs frequent, shallow watering, while trees need long, deep watering. Your alternatives are to keep the two separate, or let the grass turn brown during dry spells.

The most efficient water-saving technique is to landscape with Astro-Turf®, or green-painted asphalt. Since that's not practical, your next best option is to incorporate a ground cover such as decorative thyme, ivy, strawberry, or a legume. However, if you have playing- and ball-fields, you need grass as opposed to ground cover, and you need to water it so it can survive campers' recreational activity.

If you must water grass, shrubbery, and/or gardens, investigate these water-efficient options:

❏ **Most expensive:** An underground sprinkler system on timers, such as the type golf courses use, or buried drip lines.

A Closer Look

Xeriscaping: The practice of matching appropriate horticulture to the climate.

A Closer Look

Water gardens, trees, and landscapes on overcast days or before the heat of the day—no later than midmorning—or use a slow-running drip line or soaker hose. If you water later in the day, the sun evaporates 30 to 50 percent of the liquid, and water droplets left on leaves magnify the sunlight and burn them. In some climates, where temperatures remain high even at night, you may be able to water after the sun goes down without encouraging growths of fungus and mildew.

Because mildew hibernates in dry weather, the drier and warmer the climate, the less chance there is of harming vegetation when watering at night. Generally, if evening temperatures are above 50°F, you can water after dark without concern. If you have doubts, call your local nursery. For farm orchards and large vegetable gardens, ask your local nursery, agricultural extension agent, or horticultural professional about the most efficient watering options.

❏ **Moderately expensive:** An electronic faucet meter system (approximately $100, plus 9-volt battery). Attach it to your faucet, hook your hose and sprinkler to it, then preset your watering days and times.

❏ **Less expensive:** A mechanical faucet meter (about $30) or a mechanical measuring sprinkler. You can preset each to run a fixed amount of water, then switch off.

It generally takes a 1/2 inch to 3/4 inch of water a week, soaked into the ground, to keep lawns healthy. Generally, getting this water can be costly and a challenge throughout the year in Sun Belt states, and in summer elsewhere in North America. That is why we recommend limiting or eliminating your water-demanding lawn areas, in favor of decorative, climate-specific ornamental bushes and flowering plants.

Everyone who maintains turf and fields, however, should calculate the amount of time it will take to soak the ground enough to keep them healthy. There are two parts to this: (1) how much time it takes to get that amount of water laid down, and (2) how much time it takes for the turf and earth to absorb it.

To calculate the first part, how long you should water, place three empty cans marked inside at 3/4 inch at various distances from your sprinkler, then time how long it takes to fill each can to the mark. Add the three times together, then divide by three to determine the average. This average is the amount of time you should spend watering your camp's lawn. (This exercise is detailed as a camper activity in Chapter 3.)

To calculate the second part, how fast your soil absorbs water, dig out a sample of it, pour a sample into a 1-quart mason jar, and pour a cup of water on top. With a watch, time how long the soil takes to absorb the moisture to a depth of 1 inch. If it is within your original watering time, no adjustment is necessary. If it takes longer, however, you may have to water longer to get the water "deep enough" to be worthwhile.

Your local nursery, agricultural extension agent, or horticultural professional can give you even more specific information. It factors your faucet flow rate (which you have already calculated), the diameter and length of your hose line, the type of sprinkler, and the area to water, then tells you how long to run the sprinklers for adequate coverage.

OTHER OUTDOOR WATER USAGE

Lawns and gardens are not the only outdoor places where camps waste water. The following activities are often overlooked in water conservation programs. (Use Worksheet 5-4: Outdoor Faucet Use, and Worksheet 5-5: Leaking Faucet Water Waste to figure current use and possible dollar savings.)

❏ Many camps hose down roads, walkways, and decks as part of their cleaning procedures. Substitute push broom sweeping.

❏ Most people were taught to wash vehicles by spraying them with water. Instead, use a five-gallon bucket of water with a biodegradable soap and chamois, soft cloth, or soft brush. Do not leave a hose running. If you need hose water, use a nozzle and keep it shut off when you're not spraying. To rinse the vehicle, use two or three more bucketsful. Only then should you turn on the hose for a final touchup rinse.

❏ Outdoor spigots that leak water can remain undetected for long periods of time, since you rarely hear the accompanying dripping sound. Check all outdoor spigots for leaks and repair where needed.

RE-EXAMINE YOUR DRINKING FOUNTAINS

Program Idea

Talk about how wasteful water fights can be. Ask campers to brainstorm ways to have fun with water without wasting it.

Half of the water that comes out of a drinking fountain spigot runs right past the mouth and down the drain. You can get a rough estimate of how much water you waste at fountains by assuming that each member of your camp population takes four drinks a day, wasting three ounces at each trip. Use Worksheet 5-6: Drinking Fountain Water Use to calculate the dollar savings potential for your camp.

To save water, encourage your staff and campers to carry water bottles. It is an adventurous image that easily translates into a fashion statement: bottles strapped to belts or set in fanny packs like explorers' canteens.

Ask parents to include water bottles or canteens in the equipment list you send to your incoming participants, and then sell water bottles at the camp trading post to staff and campers who didn't bring one.

WATER-SAVER'S CHART

The following chart provides the average amount of water used in daily camp activities, how to cut down on that amount, and potential savings per task.

Thanks go to the Calleguas (California) Municipal Water District who originally designed the chart for residential users.

ACTION	NORMAL USE	CONSERVATION USE
Shower	Water running (Average 5 minutes: 25–37 gallons)	Wet down, soap up, rinse off (Average 2 minutes: 10–15 gallons)
Tub bath	Fill tub: (20–35 gallons)	Limit level: (7–10 gallons)
Wash hands	Tap running (2–3 gallons)	Fill basin, rinse (1 gallon)
Brush teeth	Tap running (10 gallons)	Wet brush, brief rinse (1/2 gallon)
Shave	Tap running (20 gallons)	Fill basin (1 gallon)
Toilet flush	Tank sizes vary (5–7 gallons)	Water displacement bottle (4.5–6.5 gallons)

Washer	Full cycle, top (60 gallons)	Short cycle, minimum level (27 gallons)
Outdoor watering or hose down	Average hose (10 gallons/minute)	Use hose nozzle (50 percent less water); Use push broom (no water use)
Wash car	Hose running (10 minutes = 100 gallons)	Bucket and hose rinse (20 gallons)

FINAL THOUGHTS

Camps that don't evaluate their water usage are not only contributing to an environmental shortage, they're pouring dollars down the drain. By following the guidelines in this chapter and filling out the accompanying worksheets, you can improve your bottom line and reduce your impact on your ecosystem in one season.

WORKSHEET 5–1
TOILET TANK DISPLACERS

Toilet Tank Water Usage

number of tank toilets   ———

× tank size (gallons)   ———

× average flushes per day   ———

= water use per day (gallons)   ———

× days per season   ———

= water use per season (gallons)   ———

Water Displacer Calculations

size of displacer (liters)   ———

× number tank toilets   ———

= water saved per flush (liters)   ———

× average flushes per day   ———

= water saved per day (liters)   ———

× days per season   ———

= water saved per season (liters)   ———

÷ liters per gallon (assume 4)   4

= water saved per season (gallons)   ———

Anticipated Water Dollar Savings

Note: In most areas of the country, water prices are charged per 100 cubic feet (748 gallons) used. This amount also is called a "unit." Check your water statement to learn how many gallons are in a unit and how prices are charged in your specific area.

water saved per season (gallons)   ———

÷ gallons per unit (748 in some areas)   ———

= water saved per season (units)   ———

× water cost per 748 gallons (unit) ($)   ———

= water dollar savings per season ($)   ———

WORKSHEET 5–2
SHOWER HEAD WATER WASTE

SHOWER HEAD WATER USAGE PER DAY	OLD STYLE	NEW STYLE
number of shower heads	———	———
× flow rate (gallons per minute per head)	———	———
× average minutes per shower	———	———
× average number of showers per day	———	———
= water use per day (gallons)	———	———

SHOWER HEAD WATER USAGE PER SEASON	OLD STYLE	NEW STYLE
water use per day (gallons)	———	———
× days per season	———	———
= water use per season (gallons)	———	———

SAVINGS

old usage per season (gallons)	———
− new usage per season (gallons)	———
= water savings per season (gallons)	———

Anticipated Water Dollar Saving

Note: In most areas of the country, water prices are charged per 100 cubic feet (748 gallons) used. This amount is also called a "unit." Check your water statement to learn how many gallons are in a unit and how prices are charged in your specific area.

water saved per season (gallons)	———
÷ 748 gallons per unit	———
= water saved per season (units)	———
× cost per water unit ($)	———
= water dollar savings per season ($)	———

WORKSHEET 5–3
WATER USE ACTION LIST

_____ Complete water usage calculations and comparisons.

_____ Is a water company conservation loan, rebate, subsidy available?

_____ Y _____ N _____ N/A _____ For what?

_____ Number of low-flow shower heads needed _____

_____ Price per head $ _____ × number heads _____ = total $ _____

_____ Total $ _____ + tax $ _____ + shipping $ _____ = $ _____

_____ Which section of the budget covers this expense _____

_____ Gallon savings _____ per season/year (from manufacturer's information).

_____ Water cost (see water company bill) $ _____ per 100 cu. ft.

_____ Dollar savings per season/year $ _____ (see Worksheet 5-2)

_____ Product supplier _____ local _____ mail order

_____ Supplier name _____

Supplier address _____

Supplier city, state, zip _____

Supplier telephone _____

_____ Delivery by _____ (date)

_____ Installation equipment needed:

    _____ adjustable wrench

    _____ teflon tape

    _____ labor: number of laborers × 12 minutes × number of heads

    _____ other _____

_____ Possible complications: _____

    _____ galvanized pipe rusted, needs rethreading or replacement. Plumber cost $ _____

    _____ pipe diameter different from shower head coupling diameter. Get threaded couplings. Cost $ _____

_____ Sell this project to the board.

WORKSHEET 5-4
OUTDOOR FAUCET USE

number faucets _____

flow rate (gpm) _____

Watering

hours/day _____

× 60 minutes/hour _____ 60

× flow rate (gpm) _____

= water use per day (gallons) _____

Road/walkway washdown

hours/day _____

× 60 minutes/hour _____ 60

× flow rate (gpm) _____

= water use per day (gallons) _____

Vehicle/equipment washdown

hours/day _____

× 60 minutes/hour _____ 60

× flow rate (gpm) _____

= water use per day (gallons) _____

Other _____

hours/day _____

× 60 minutes/hour _____ 60

× flow rate (gpm) _____

= water use per day (gallons) _____

Other _____

hours/day _____

× 60 minutes/hour _____ 60

× flow rate (gpm) _____

= water use per day (gallons) _____

Other _____

hours/day   _____

× 60 minutes/hour   60

× flow rate (gpm)   _____

= water use per day (gallons)   _____

Other _____

hours/day   _____

× 60 minutes/hour   60

× flow rate (gpm)   _____

= water use per day (gallons)   _____

Total Daily Use

add all tasks' water use per day (gallons)   _____

× days/camp season   _____

= total water use per season (gallons)   _____

Current Total Outdoor Water Cost

water cost per unit ($)   _____

× total use per season (gallons)   _____

÷ 748 gallons/unit   _____

= total water cost per season ($)   _____

Reducing Outdoor Faucet Use

Road/walkway wash-down: use push brooms instead

Assume the average lifetime of a push broom is three years.

push broom cost ($)   _____

× number push brooms   _____

= total cost for brooms ($)   _____

water dollar savings over three years ($)   _____

− total cost for brooms ($)   _____

= total cost savings ($)   _____

Vehicle/equipment wash-down with bucket system (see above):

Assume bucket and brush lifetime of four years.

bucket and brush cost ($)   _____

× number of buckets and brushes   _____

= total cost for buckets and brushes ($)   _____

water cost savings over four years ($)   _____

− total for buckets and brushes ($)   _____

= total savings ($)   _____

Other_____ Replace
with _____

Assume equipment lifetime of _____ years. Therefore figure savings over _____ years.

equipment cost ($)   _____

× units equipment   _____

= total cost for equipment ($)   _____

water cost savings over _____ years ($)   _____

− total cost for equipment ($)   _____

= total cost savings ($)   _____

Other_____ Replace
with _____

Assume equipment lifetime of _____ years. Therefore figure savings over _____ years.

equipment cost ($)   _____

× units equipment   _____

= total cost for equipment ($)   _____

water cost savings over _____ years ($)   _____

− total cost for equipment ($)   _____

= total cost savings ($)   _____

WORKSHEET 5–5
LEAKING FAUCET WATER WASTE

To demonstrate how quickly you are losing water, put a quart container under the faucet and time how long it takes to fill. Usually, a drip costs you 2 to 30 gallons a day. The cures: turn off dripping faucets and put new washers in those that leak.

faucet gallons per minute	————
× hours in a day	————
× days in a week (or season)	————
÷ (4) quarts in a gallon	4
= number of gallons wasted in a week (season)	————

WORKSHEET 5-6
DRINKING FOUNTAIN WATER USE

number campers	_____
× number fountains	_____
× average ounces per drink	7
× average drinks per day	4
= average water use per day (ounces)	_____
÷ 164 ounces per gallon	164
= average water use per day (gallons)	_____
÷ 748 gallons per unit	748
= average water use per day (units)	_____
× cost per unit	_____
= average cost for water use ($)	_____

Drinking Fountain Water Waste

number of camp fountains	_____
× number camp participants	_____
× average ounces water wasted per drink	3
× average drinks per day	4
= average wasted water per day (ounces)	_____
÷ 164 ounces per gallon	164
= average wasted water per day (gallons)	_____
÷ 748 gallons per unit	748
= average water use per day (units)	_____
× cost per unit	_____
= average cost of wasted water ($)	_____

6

ENERGY CONSERVATION

Using an external energy source to do useful work is one of the main features that distinguishes humans from most other animals.
—William Cunningham and Barbara Saigo, *Environmental Science: A Global Concern*

Writing in *The Efficient House Sourcebook* (Rocky Mountain Institute), Robert Sardinsky asserts that each year, conservation efforts throughout North America now "deliver" 40 percent more energy than the oil industry, and they do it more cheaply. Since 1979, millions of individual decisions to save energy have given this country more than ten times as much new energy as all net expansions of energy supply combined, he adds.

The precise figures for these claims have been tabulated by the Rocky Mountain Institute of Snowmass, Colorado. Its founder, Amory Lovins, suggests we look at wasted energy as a reserve we can tap now. "Start drilling for oil under Detroit," he often says, noting that the U.S. today imports more than 50 percent of its oil.

These are also the reasons electric utilities are now selling conservation rather than new power: they make a profit as they avoid the costs of building new power plants. Your camp can share this windfall.

ENERGY ECONOMICS

Most people take energy sources—coal, oil, gas, and electricity—for granted. So to put the difficulty of getting energy and its accompanying

A Closer Look

Wood fires in natural areas scar landscapes, deplete soil of future nutrients by interfering with the detritus cycle (the natural composting cycle), and generally alter native flora and fauna life cycles. Along this line, the American Camping Association recommends that while on a hike or campout, you use wood only as a last resort to fuel cooking or program fires. If the park where you camp does not provide wood or you don't find it in abundance at your feet, use another fuel source. Avoid depleting the area's natural resources.

A Closer Look

According to the U.S. Department of Energy, 39 percent of America's electricity today is generated by oil-fired plants, 25 percent by natural gas, 23 percent by coal, 8 percent by hydro-electric dams, 5 percent by nuclear plants, and less than 1 percent by garbage incinerators, wind, solar, land-fill methane, and other.

cost into perspective, try splitting and stacking enough cords of wood to heat your home and prepare all of your family's meals for an entire winter. After several hard days' work, you'll want to conserve the wood because you know the faster it goes, the faster you'll have to chop more.

Yet even though wood cutting depletes the world's biomass, it may be less harmful on the environment overall to cook with wood fires than fossil fuel stoves. Consider the environmental and dollar costs to extract, transport, distill, package, and distribute coal, gas, and oil fuels; build hydroelectric dams, nuclear plants, and trash incinerators; and contend with the pollution and ozone-depleting gasses they generate. Add the costs for mining, manufacturing, distributing, and maintaining the world's fuel-dependent vehicles, appliances, equipment, and industries. Whether we use wood, fossil, or nuclear energy, we deplete the Earth's biomass and ozone, pollute the land, and contribute to skin cancers and the possibility of a Greenhouse Effect caused by over-abundant atmospheric carbon dioxide. These costs may outweigh the life cycle costs of wood as a fuel.

So, how can your camp positively influence these and other energy problems? Consider every act of energy conservation as an investment in your future. Minimize you camp's demands on resources. In the long term, this approach will save you money also.

The least expensive energy options are natural gas, propane, and hydro-electricity, depending on where you live in the country. In most states, you can plug into natural gas or propane for cooking, space and water heating, and even no-CFC air conditioning. On the other hand, nuclear energy is the most expensive option, followed by coal, then oil.

The latest clashes in the Middle East have only emphasized how oil prices will continue to rise into the next century. The United States imports over half of its supplies from overseas, and will continue to do so unless Congress passes proactive energy legislation or Americans take things into their own hands and move to alternative energy systems. If the costs of oil-related wars do not show up as price increases at the gas pump, they impact your federal taxes.

Nuclear and coal prices also are increasing. Nuclear energy has been nearly driven out of business by problems with design, waste disposal, accidents (and the threat of accidents), and costs related to sealing old reactors and radioactive materials to render their radiation harmless. Environmental laws have caught up with the uranium and coal mining industries, too, and with construction and operation of coal-fired plants.

The cost of hydro-electricity is on the way up, too. During any drought year, there is less water behind dams and thus less power and higher prices. In the Northwest, dams and their turbines have endangered migrating salmon, so power-generating companies will have to invest in dam refits to protect the fish.

Natural gas and propane are the only fuels whose prices probably will remain stable (they've been depressed in the early 1990s) since the United States has domestic reserves of these fuels. Likewise, methane is becoming a viable resource: In the U.S., there are now more than 160 solid waste utilities in the country creating methane-generated electricity from landfills. In Brussels, Belgium, the Société Jean Pain is doing breakthrough work in small-scale methane generation from compost.

Things are also looking up on other fronts. Several companies are exploring the feasibility of hydrogen as a general-purpose fuel, and the Real Goods alternative energy company of Ukiah, California, has now "unhooked" thousands of homes from power grids, making them "energy independent" with a combination of solar, low-head hydro, wind, and conservation technologies and these are only some of the energy changes now afoot. Consultants at think tanks such as the Rocky Mountain Institute assert that most of America's energy demand for the next two decades can be supplied by conservation technologies that are currently available.

A TREASURE HUNT

Innovative thinking is the continuing premise of this workbook, so you are invited now to rethink the ways your camp uses your energy. Think of it as a treasure hunt: the more improvements you make, the more energy efficient your operation will be, and the more money you will save in the long run.

A Closer Look

States, too, are developing their own energy-efficiency laws. So far, California (with Title 24); Washington, Oregon, Idaho (Northwestern Power Planning Council); New York, and Massachusetts are the leaders in this direction. Others are following suit, as are some local building codes.

Moving now to energy-efficient systems also keeps you ahead of coming codes and regulations and reduces your vulnerability to rate increases and power restrictions. Congress, for example, is wrestling with energy legislation that proposes lighting standards that could make whole classes of today's inefficient incandescent lamps obsolete.

Federal, state, provincial, and local governments and energy (gas and electric) utilities now offer energy management incentives and make resources available to you, often at no charge. Contact these resources for in-depth information:

- ❏ Local utilities,
- ❏ Regional planning agencies,
- ❏ Local and state government agencies, such as the city energy office and state energy extension service,
- ❏ Federal power authorities, such as Bonneville Power Administration and Tennessee Valley Authority,
- ❏ Lighting and electrical materials suppliers,
- ❏ Energy consultants (by referral, or in the *Yellow Pages*),
- ❏ Local libraries.

Do your own reading on these subjects from the recommended reading list in Appendix A so you can ask informed questions.

WHERE TO BEGIN

No activity will succeed without direction and support from the top: your camp's administration. Again, you may create a separate mission statement about energy conservation or combine this policy with your water policy in a single statement.

You can make this declaration general, but it's more effective overall if you state specific goals, then update the goals and the statement as you achieve them. The following sample demonstrates the latter strategy:

"At Camp _____, we conserve our energy resources. As our camp policy, we:

❑ Shut off lights, appliances, and other electrical items when we're not using them;

❑ Set thermostats on air conditioners at 78°F, water heaters at 110°–130°F, and space heaters at 68°F to save energy;

❑ Use energy-efficient alternatives wherever we can, such as fans instead of air conditioners for cooling, and clotheslines instead of dryers for laundry;

❑ We welcome any suggestions from our board, staff, and campers on other ways we can conserve energy and continue creating a great camping experience for everyone."

But in order to set specific goals—for example, reducing your lighting energy demand by 40 percent this year—you need to know where you are using energy, how much it costs, and where you can make improvements and reductions.

ENERGY BILLING

First, collect your camp's energy bills over the past year. Use worksheets 6-1, 6-2, and 6-3 at the end of this chapter to help you figure yearly use and average monthly use for these utilities. These worksheets also help you identify seasonal usage trends and costs. Save copies of the worksheets from this year and compare them to worksheets you complete after you begin taking energy-saving steps.

Most electric utilities figure energy use and charges in kilowatt hours (kwh) with one thousand watts equaling one kilowatt. It takes 657,000 watt hours of energy, or 657 kwh, to light a 75-watt light bulb 24 hours a day for one year. (75 watts × 24 hours/day × 365 days/year = 657,000 watt hours/year or 657 kwh.)

Oil suppliers determine the use and charges for petroleum products by the gallon. It takes 63 gallons of oil in an oil-fired power plant to light a 75-watt light bulb for a year.

Natural gas is supplied by the hundred cubic feet (CCF) and charged by the Therm, or gas energy content, in British Thermal Units (Btus). There are 100,000 Btus in one Therm, and it takes one Btu to raise the temperature of a pound of water one degree Fahrenheit. The gas company multiplies your month's usage in CCF by its Btu factor. (The Btu factor varies slightly with the quality of gas, which is tested at the company's receiving point.) That value is multiplied by the dollar rate the energy company charges. It takes 59 cubic feet of gas in a natural gas-fired turbine plant to light a 75-watt light bulb for a year.

LIGHTING

One of the easiest ways to save energy and related costs is to manage the electricity your lighting uses by turning off unused lights and changing to lower-wattage bulbs. To know how much you could be saving, determine how much energy you currently use to light your facility.

Begin by counting *all* of your lights including the entrance, dining hall, office(s), cabins, conference room(s), bathrooms, storage, shop, and receiving area. You may have one or several types of lights in each area. Count them all: And don't forget signs, spotlights, and other sources besides room lighting, no matter how little you use them. Always note the wattage of each bulb as you make your rounds. (For fluorescents, use the wattage on the ballasts, not the bulbs themselves.)

Now, use Worksheet 6-4: Lighting Inventory to figure how much energy is being used by your facility's current lighting. This task helps you become aware of your usage patterns for lights, and the periods of time during the day and night that you use them.

Once you complete the lighting worksheet, compare these totals to the total electricity amounts charged to your monthly electric bill to see what percentage of your electricity goes to lighting your facility. There are a number of options for reducing this percentage and, therefore, your total electric bill. They include:

❑ Lamp options,

❑ Fixture options,

❑ Dimmers, sensors, and switches.

LAMPS You may be using any of several types of lights: incandescent, fluorescent, mercury or sodium vapor, and halogen. Incandescent bulbs are most widely used for general and spot lighting in homes and businesses (see Figure 6-1). Inside the bulb is a filament—a fine tungsten wire that is stretched between two

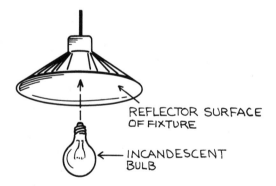

REFLECTOR SURFACE OF FIXTURE

INCANDESCENT BULB

Figure 6-1. Incandescent bulb and fixture

wires inside the bulb. When electricity passes through the filament, the tungsten resists it and becomes "white hot," producing the light that you see. You can see a similar event happen when you turn on an electric stove, except the burner becomes "red hot."

Fluorescents operate by an electric ballast igniting a rare Earth vapor (mercury) and coating (phosphor) in the globe or tube. Fluorescents give diffuse, not spot, lighting (see Figure 6-2). Fluorescents are available in

A Closer Look

Fluorescents last longer in general than incandescents, so you don't need to buy and replace them as often. The return on investment for your camp in avoided costs can be 15 percent to 20 percent— better rates than a bank, CD, or bond can offer!

A Closer Look

CFs last 10 to 13 times longer than conventional incandescent bulbs and use up to 90 percent less energy than incandescents. According to research done by the Rocky Mountain Institute, CFs keep half a ton of CO_2 (generated by fossil fuel-burning power plants) out of the atmosphere over their lifetimes.

tube and bulb-style lamps. Mercury- and sodium-vapor lamps also work on ballast ignition.

Fluorescents are generally more expensive than incandescents, so view them as a long-term investment. Compare the benefit you get from spending an extra $1.50 per lamp for a T-8 (1-inch diameter tube) instead of a T-12 (1 1/2-inch diameter tube). Over the life of these lamps, the

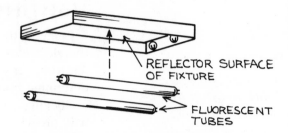

Figure 6-2. Fluorescent bulb and fixture

T-8s cut your lighting energy cost by 35 percent to 40 percent. The life-span of a fluorescent tube is about 10,000 hours (up to several years) depending on how many times it's activated and its original manufacturing quality.

But before buying fluorescents, you should understand the following compatibility cautions.

Compact fluorescents (CFs) cannot replace incandescent bulbs in most floor and table lamps or in enclosed fixtures designed for incandescent bulbs. The CF globes, tubes, and bases are most often larger than standard incandescents too, so before you buy, make certain your fixture accommodates its height and width, and that the socket diameter matches its base. Some lighting stores offer kits to retrofit fixtures to accommodate fluorescents.

CFs are available in two styles: as a bulb unit fused to the ballast and as a ballast with a replaceable lamp. The ballast is good for the lifetimes of four or five lamps, so CFs sold as bulb-ballast units aren't necessarily a good deal. It is usually recommended you purchase the CF style with the ballast separate from the replaceable lamps.

As of 1992, there are two CF ballast types: magnetic and electronic. Magnetic ballasts have an iron core with copper wire wound around it, and they operate at standard electricity: 60 cycles per second, or hertz (Hz). They sometimes hum in standard sockets. Electronic ballasts have a solid-state chip that converts the standard 60 cycle current to 20,000 cycles. They are more efficient, produce less heat, and are generally silent in standard sockets.

Humming is the standard complaint about CFs. This noise is caused by the ballast, the fixture, or both. A 60-cycle magnetic ballast compact lamp will likely hum in a standard fixture, and its light may even flicker annoyingly. To avoid this, buy CFs with ballasts that run above 20,000 cycles. If you still get humming with one of the higher cycle, ask your lighting supplier about retrofitting or changing your fixture.

The light quality of fluorescents is another common complaint. The North American public is used to the warm yellow glow of incandescent light bulbs. Both warm (yellow) and cold (white) spectrum CFs have been available since they were introduced, yet their manufacturers for some reason marketed the cold spectrum lights first. Consequently, the public has a negative view of CFs: "They hum, and it looks like we're in a rest area bathroom!" is the standard line. Specify the warm spectrum models from your supplier, or discuss mixing the two to maintain the desired light levels and still preserve a warmly lit atmosphere. Some compact models can be dimmed, so if you require that, check with your lighting specialist.

Some people express concern about pollution possibilities from the phosphors and mercury in fluorescent lamps when they are discarded. The phosphors dissipate in the environment, combining with other elements, but the mercury remains and builds up. To date, solid waste managers and environmentalists are giving their blessing to the lamps because the quantity of mercury is tiny, and a single fluorescent uses so much less energy and lasts up to 10 times longer than a single incandescent.

To offset CFs extra cost, you throw out only 1 compact fluorescent for every 10 incandescents you replace and throw out, and they require 90 percent less storage space, too. On balance, fluorescents appear to be a great deal. And rest assured, manufacturers such as Philips and GE are feverishly working to devise a mercury-free lamp.

Halogen bulbs are another alternative to incandescents. (Halogen and halogen quartz are terms used interchangeably.) These bulbs are similar to incandescents in that they have a tungsten filament inside the bulb. However, halogen bulbs also contain a halogen gas, usually iodine or bromine, that helps keep the tungsten filament molecules from evaporating over time. This allows them a longer life—almost double that of conventional incandescents. The filament can operate at a higher, or brighter, temperature and greater efficiency.

Halogen bulbs are designed for spot lighting, and can be used as a direct replacement for incandescents. They're generally smaller than incandescents but have efficient reflector designs built in to supply the same brightness (see Figure 6-3). A standard 60- to 90-watt halogen supplies the same lighting brightness, or lumens, as a 150-watt incandescent.

Watt for watt, a halogen's heat output is greater than an incandescent's. However, a lower-watt halogen can replace a higher-watt incandescent, and produce the same light with equal or less total heat output. In a typical incandescent, 93 to 94 percent of the watts are heat output and 6 to 7 percent are light. In a halogen, 83 to 85 percent of the watts go to heat and 15 to 17 percent go to light.

Halogens last even longer if you operate them

Warning

If you are offered cheap lights or cheap fluorescent ballasts from a company you don't know, turn them down. Quality of the units, their light outputs, and longevity are all suspect.

A Closer Look

As added incentive, your local electric utility may pay you a rebate for the lower-wattage lamps to help offset the cost of buying and installing them. Some even conduct free "energy assessments" for you.

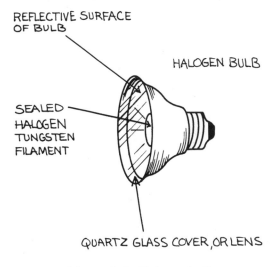

REFLECTIVE SURFACE OF BULB

HALOGEN BULB

SEALED HALOGEN TUNGSTEN FILAMENT

QUARTZ GLASS COVER, OR LENS

Figure 6-3. Halogen bulb

at less than full power. Use a dimmer to turn down the power. This trick may not work as well with incandescents, because dropping power on them can cause a spectrum shift to a dimmer or more yellow, dingy light quality. Halogen light is so brilliant that shifting it down a notch actually warms up the quality.

FIXTURES As mentioned earlier, you may have to change fixtures to accommodate some lighting upgrades. Whenever you change lights, you nearly always want to maintain or improve lighting quality in terms of lumen outputs and color. This can become a complex endeavor.

Lumen values and color qualities change throughout a day and the seasons as the quality of daylight entering your buildings changes. The quality and color of artificial lighting can be varied with direct and indirect designs, reflectors, and mixing different lamp types.

To explore this in detail, and begin retrofitting, consult a lighting expert. You can find local experts through your lighting suppliers and contractors, your electric utility, and the *Yellow Pages* under "Lighting." Offer the information from the lighting worksheets at the end of the chapter to help the expert decide the best plan for your camp areas.

DIMMERS, SENSORS, AND SWITCHES Motion and light sensors, timers, and trip switches turn lights on only when they are actually needed, and therefore save a tremendous amount of energy. Millions of people use these devices in their homes to switch lights and appliances on and off automatically at preset times.

Again, you can buy these sensors, timers, and trip switches at most electronic and hardware stores, and install them yourself in rooms and areas that get infrequent use. Computer programs now available also enable you to centralize the control of these electric devices from your office or office PC.

MACHINES AND APPLIANCES

Because machines and appliances use energy, they are excellent candidates for your energy conservation efforts. And these machines generally have long lifespans, so the financial rewards are greater, too. When you look at any machine, appliance, or piece of equipment, consider its benefits over its entire life.

As an example, a copy machine works by using a step-up transformer to boost incoming voltage (110V–120V) to 10,000V, so the rotating drum inside can be static-electrically charged and hold the toner particles. When it lays these particles on the paper, the paper is heat- and pressure-treated at approximately 400°F using a 550- to 700-watt lamp to bond the toner. Thus, using a copy machine draws a lot of energy and is expensive.

The following simple comparison of life cycle costs for two copy machines, taken from *Energy Management Workbooks for Local Governments* produced by the Puget Sound (Washington) Council of Governments and the Bonneville Power Administration, can be applied to any appliance or piece of equipment.

Warning

Convert from incandescents to halogens only in ceramic sockets, or those which do not carry the warning "Use no more than 60W (or 75W) bulb in this fixture." These lamps have paper sockets and can catch fire in the high heat contact of halogen bulbs.

	INITIAL COST BASIS		LIFE CYCLE FIVE-YEAR COST	
	MACHINE A	MACHINE B	MACHINE A	MACHINE B
Purchase price	$800	$500	$800	$500
Energy operating cost	$200/yr	$300/yr	$1,000	$1,500
Maintenance cost	$40/yr	$50/yr	$200	$250
Total			$2,000	$2,250

This example assumes constant dollars. Over the depreciation period, machine A costs less than machine B, but people often ignore the energy savings and repair costs when they look at initial cost. Generally, the better-built machine is less expensive to operate.

Potential Pitfall

Every item you purchase is an investment, so beware of always hunting for the lowest bid on equipment and services. Always consider energy costs to operate the equipment, use accounting methods that consider the life of the machine, and you will likely make a more sound investment decision.

A Closer Look

Every 10° you set back the temperature can reduce your water heating energy by up to 6 percent.

WATER HEATERS Between 5 and 20 percent of the water your camp uses passes through water heaters, and as much as 40 percent of your total energy bill goes to heat that water, according to Seattle City Light of Seattle, Washington.

So one quick, easy way to save energy is to wash and rinse items with cold water whenever possible. Another is to turn down heater thermostats for your water.

In locations where you can draw on natural gas or propane energy sources, you may consider the long-term savings achievable by replacing tank-style water heaters with on-demand water heaters, which only "fire-up" to make hot water when you turn on the tap. Invented in Europe where energy prices are prohibitively high, several brands of these on-demand heaters are making their ways across the Atlantic. However, there are drawbacks: They are expensive to buy, and so may not provide you with the life cycle savings offered by tank units. Also, some produce carbon monoxide as a gas combustion by-product, so the heater must be placed in a well-ventilated space.

An insulating jacket around the heater and a wrap-on hot water piping can reduce the energy you use to heat water by up to 50 percent. However, a sealed jacket can cause overheating and premature tank failure. To avoid this, make holes in the jacket so it does not cover access panels to thermostats, heating elements, or junction box; external wiring; operating instructions or labels; or air vents on top of gas heaters.

To further boost efficiency, drain off sediment-laden water through the valve at the bottom of the tank every two months. For larger than household-sized units, ask for your water or energy utility's advice.

Use Worksheet 6–5 at the end of this chapter to track your camp's efforts to make water heaters more efficient.

HEATING AND AIR CONDITIONING Most of North America's heating, ventilation, and air conditioning systems (HVACs) are not

A Closer Look

The American Camping Association's Standards for Day and Resident Camps recommends that you set water heater temperatures no higher than 110°F to protect adults and children from scalding when washing and showering. The exception to this suggestion is your kitchen water heater, which can be set only as low as 130°F and still supply adequate temperature water for the dishwasher. Check with your local health department, however, to make certain that a 130° setting complies with the health code.

A Closer Look

Every degree you turn back on forced air heater thermostats can mean a 3 percent heat energy savings over 24 hours.

Warning

You need to consult with a utility auditor or an HVAC engineer to discover if you can substitute variable speed motors at your camp. Ask your local utility, your state energy extension office, or look in the Yellow Pages for a qualified engineer.

well-maintained. As a result, they operate at dramatically reduced efficiencies, which means they deliver relatively little performance for the energy they use. By keeping heating and air-conditioning units "tuned" and their filters cleaned, you can save up to five percent of operating expenses, plus reduce emissions from heaters that run on oil and gas.

"Tuning" involves cleaning filters about once a month when units are in regular operation, lubricating and maintaining machinery, and keeping motors and ductwork clear of dust, grit, and soot.

The Rocky Mountain Institute estimates that in the United States alone, electric motors use more energy, on a Btu basis, than all U.S. vehicles combined. A standard commercial motor in its first year of operation, for example, can use energy amounting to 10 times its original cost. An antidote to this where you have a variable load (ask your utility) is a variable speed drive motor, which can run at less power, and use much less energy. In some cases, a variable speed motor running at 50 percent power uses 87 percent less electrical energy than a standard motor at full power.

Other ways to reduce the energy that your heaters and air conditioners use include setting back the thermostat at night, insulating buildings appropriately, maintaining regular maintenance schedules on equipment, replacing current thermostats with more efficient ones, and adding fans to keep air moving. Use the worksheets at the end of the chapter to help you check equipment and schedule repairs for your camp.

As you improve your current heating and air conditioning, the next step is to refine the types of systems and energy sources you use. For instance, your facility may have an oil furnace, which probably heats at 62 percent efficiency (oil converted to usable heat) and sends an 800°F exhaust up the chimney flue. This may not matter to you if your facility operates primarily in summer and you rarely use the heater. But if your camp operates in cooler weather or year-round, you may want to consider upgrading that heater.

If the heater is a pre-1975 model and in good shape, you can change its burner to a flame retention unit, which costs under $1,000 installed (1992 price on residential-sized units). This can boost heating efficiency from the original 62 percent to between 66 and 70 percent, reduce exhaust temperature to 550°F, and reduce your fuel costs by 5 to 10 percent. Or, you may want to replace the old oil furnace with a new, high-efficiency one, which runs more efficiently (70–74 percent) but still wastes 500°F of heat as exhaust.

If you are served by natural gas lines, consider replacing the oil furnace with a new gas unit. Models are available that operate at up to 94 percent efficiency, and exhaust 110°F of heat. Though installation cost can be high (up to $2,500 per 3,000 square-foot building), the operating cost is generally half that of oil. You should recoup your investment in 5 to 10 years.

If you cannot get natural gas, check on the availability of propane. If you find a local supplier, determine the costs and paybacks for installing a propane-supplied tank and gas furnace(s) for your camp. You may find it has an advantage over oil.

For space heating, there's always electric overhead and baseboard heat. These are economical only where electricity is inexpensive. To examine this option, call an energy auditor from your local utility or local or state energy extension service to conduct a survey at your camp.

Generally, upgrades can be quite expensive initially. But if they boost efficiency and reduce your long-term energy demand and costs, they are always an environmentally and financially sound choice. The key questions to ask are whether the upgrade will pay you back, and over how long a period. Upgrades enable you to get the same warmth with less energy input, and limited seasonal use means less total use, and therefore, longer system life.

If you are approaching this strictly from a cost-benefit standpoint, you may use the heater too seldom during your season to make this an economical investment. Supplementary money may be available, however. Call your local utility or state energy office to ask if it offers rebates and/or low- or zero-interest loans for those who purchase "qualifying" high-efficiency heating units.

TAKE ADVANTAGE OF SOLAR If you are in a sunny climate—generally between 35° north and south latitude receive more than 3,000 hours of sunshine per year—strongly consider using solar units to supplement your water, space, and pool heating. North of 35° latitude, there are marked seasonal variations in sunshine, but you may still be able to effectively use it to your advantage. Even in the Arctic, the sun's intensity is high enough in summer to power solar systems; winter there is another story, however.

Solar panels and systems vary widely in price (see Appendix A for catalog particulars) but are worth considering in light of how much it may save you in future energy costs. Check, too, with your local solar systems supplier in the *Yellow Pages*.

REFRIGERATORS AND FREEZERS Institutional walk-in refrigerators and freezers are large, expensive items that are usually well-built and well-insulated. To keep them running at peak efficiency, however, here are a few items to check:

❑ Operating temperatures: First, check the thermostat settings. Each locality's health department legally mandates the maximum safe temperatures for refrigerators and freezers. Generally, the maximum range for freezers is 0° to +5°F; for refrigerators, 38° to 40°F, but ask your health inspector to be certain. The closer you run to the high side allowed by health codes, the less energy your coolers use.

❑ Door seals: Over time, door latches, hinges, and gaskets wear and stop sealing in the cold. This also makes it easier for users to leave doors open enough to suck in heat from outside and rob energy. Look for visible openings at the door seal (where you can feel the cold), condensation on the insides of doors and refrigerator walls, or door condensation and thin layers of ice on the freezers. If these symptoms appear, call your maintenance person to make repairs.

A Closer Look

On swimming pools, use a black or clear plastic bubble blanket to cover the water and provide solar heat. For lap swimming pools, divide the blanket in half or quarters, lengthwise, to uncover only the lanes or sections you want to use. Then, re-cover the pool at the end of the day to retain heat.

❏ Structural joint seals: Same principle as door seals; look for the condensation or a thin sheet of ice and call your maintenance person.

Use common sense when using these items. Open a refrigerator or freezer door briefly, get what you want, then close the door. When you're ready to stock these storage areas, stack everything outside so you leave the door propped open for as short a span as possible.

STOVES AND OVENS Like refrigerators and freezers, institutional stoves and ovens are built to last. But to keep them running efficiently, again you need to check for the following conditions:

❏ Operating temperatures: First, check that oven thermostat settings match the heat generated inside. Every oven cooks "hot" or "cold," that is, above or below the temperature on the dial, and every cook can get used to that. But why bother? Set a thermometer inside the oven, and if the heat isn't on the mark, call a repair person to reset it. This reduces wasted energy and food.

❏ Door seals: As with refrigerators and freezers, door latches, hinges, and gaskets wear out over time. The most obvious thing to feel for is escaping heat. Other evidence would be a visible shot gasket or damaged hinge. Again, call your repair person to fix it.

❏ Structural joint seals: Same principle as door seals. Look for cracks at the joints, feel the heat, and then have them repaired.

Again, use common sense when using these appliances. Open an oven door briefly, get what you want, then close the door. When you're ready to put multiple dishes in the oven, arrange the pans close by outside so you only need the door open a very short time. On an electric stove, the burners retain heat even after they've been turned off, so turn off the burner before cooking is finished. Also, cook several things, one after the other on the same burner when possible.

Convection ovens use the same energy as standard ovens, but circulate the heat to reduce cooking times for certain dishes. Check a convection oven cookbook to determine how much cooking time and energy this style oven can save your camp.

DISHWASHERS There are two types of institutional dishwashers: low-temperature and high-temperature. High-temp units wash with 180° to 185°F water, which sterilizes dishware and leaves it so hot, it air-dries quickly. The units are designed with electric water heat boosters, either built-in or as companion items. To work best, they must have 130° to 140°F water entering from the kitchen water heater. Low-temp units wash at 130° to 140°F and use a chlorinated sanitizing agent in the rinse. Also consider these similarities and differences:

❏ Soap and water: Both types use the same type of soap, the same amount of water for wash and rinse cycles—one to two gallons—and both run on either 220V or 115V, depending on the model.

❏ Hard water: High-temp units using hard water can precipitate out minerals or ore on the dishware, leaving a powdery residue (whitish or grayish if mineral, reddish if ore) that requires extra cleaning. Low-temp units don't.

❑ Septic systems: Both types can be used with septic systems. The low-temp chemical rinse contains 50 parts per million (ppm) chlorine (drinking water contains one ppm), but this dissipates within five minutes of exposure to air, heat, and solids.

❑ Water savings: Both high- and low-temp systems recycle clean rinse water into wash water for the next load.

❑ Effectiveness: As long as the high-temp unit's wash water runs consistently at 180° to 185°F, it's as effective as the low-temp.

For specific answers, call local restaurant suppliers, or have them refer you to a dishwasher specialist.

BUILDINGS

A Closer Look

Camp structures are often rustic, striking a balance between modern conveniences and the spirit of roughing it. But no matter how rustic the look and feel of the buildings, those where people gather daily—dining halls, activity buildings, classrooms, the infirmary—should be as energy efficient as possible.

In many cases, your camp buildings were built long before the present administration was in charge. Yet although you may have had little or no say in how the buildings were designed and where they were placed, you do have a say in how well you use the camp's man-made facilities today.

You can assess building energy management yourself with formulas and worksheets available from your state department of energy or energy extension service, but this is a complex process. You'll have to factor in numbers of doors, placements of windows, climate humidity, ceiling heights, and numbers of people who use the building. Among other things, you need to know that each human puts off the heat of a 100–watt incandescent light bulb, so a group generates a lot of warmth.

It's easier to call your local gas or utility company and have a representative do the assessment for free. Based on that information, you can evaluate the costs and savings of insulation and more efficient operating systems.

No matter how efficient your building is, consider the following energy-saving ideas for heating and cooling:

❑ Caulk or double-pane windows, particularly those that face north, away from the sun.

❑ Insulate ceilings, walls, and floors to keep in the heat and coolness.

❑ Use ceiling, window, and exhaust fans instead of air conditioning units to move air and withdraw heat. To distribute heat more efficiently, use ceiling and heatalator fans. (Sealed bearing fans use less energy and need less maintenance than belt-driven fans.) As a substitute for costly air conditioning, use window fans, and arrange wall and window openings to create paths for the air to flow all the way through each building.

❑ Wrap heating and cooling ducts with insulation.

❑ Turn up air conditioner thermostats. "Cool" can be achieved by dropping eight to ten degrees from ambient temperature, decreasing the humidity, or both.

❏ Try swamp coolers (humidifying heat pumps). They add humidity and are good for cooling in the arid climates of mountain and desert areas.

❏ Investigate heat pumps. Be warned, however: They tend to be expensive ($2,000 to $3,000 installed, 1991 price), bulky, and noisy, and may not realize any payback for you. The most common type, finned air-to-air models, can be poor performers if temperatures fall to freezing or rise above 90°F. Ground source models have no cold weather problems but are expensive to install, and may not be cost-effective. Gather local opinions from your electric utility, state energy office, and HVAC expert(s) before you proceed with this option.

Programming Idea

Building primitive solar panel models as projects lets campers and staff members feel they're contributing a gift to their camp that will keep on giving.

❏ Explore using passive solar designs. In cooler climates, when you remodel or engage in new construction, arrange windows along the daily path of the sun and insulate buildings to create a cozy indoors greenhouse from solar warmth. Put extra insulation in the outside building walls that face away from the sun. To take even more advantage of solar power, make windows smaller on the cooler north and northeast sides of the buildings. Check your local building codes regarding the windows you plan to install; most codes now require all be double-paned, or double-paned and argon gas-filled.

❏ Use deciduous trees and awnings to shade sides of buildings facing the sun's path. The trees provide shade in summer and let the sun through to warm the building when they lose their leaves in winter.

❏ Use offset roof lines, skylights, and bigger windows on the southeast, south and west sides to create airiness and brightness year-round, particularly in the darker winter months, and reduce your daytime reliance on artificial, energy-demanding lights.

To prepare for your camp's energy efficiency assessment, determine which buildings you would modify first. To decide, fill out Worksheet 6–11 and consider the following questions.

❏ Is this structure currently heated and/or air conditioned?

❏ Does it need to hold heat or cold during use hours?

❏ What are its use hours? Seasons?

❏ What does it cost to heat/cool the structure?

❏ What will it take to make this structure energy efficient? New windows and frames? New doors and frames? New caulking? New roof? Finishing the walls? Adding a ceiling fan? Adding insulation?

❏ Will the money saved by insulating offset the cost of insulating? Over what period of time?

❏ Does the local government or utility have grants or low-interest loans to subsidize insulating?

❏ Can insulation materials' labor be donated, or offered at a discount that's within the budget?

Also look closely at your kitchen for wasted energy sources. Stoves, ovens, freezers, and refrigerators produce and waste heat, some of which can be channeled into useful functions. For instance, a simple reversible fan and duct system can enable you to warm the dining hall with kitchen heat in cool weather, and cool the kitchen with dining hall air in warm weather. If your refrigerators and freezers generate enough heat, it may be feasible to install a heat recovery unit and pipe the excess to supplement your water or space heater. Call your utility or HVAC expert for advice on whether this option is cost-effective for your camp.

CAMP VEHICLES

A Closer Look

To conserve energy and reduce pollution with fossil-fuel burning vehicles, go by foot, bicycle, canoe, public transport, or car/van pool when possible.

A Closer Look

Consolidate out-of-camp trips for supplies and errands, such as gathering people from airports and other locations. Post two lists on your office bulletin board: one for supply items, one for people pick-ups. Designate one driver to make only one run each day.

Last, but not least in the energy conservation equation, are the vehicles that camp staff and participants use. This list includes not only cars and trucks but also motorcycles, tractors, power boats, and any other motorized vehicles.

Start by establishing a few basic tenets about your "rolling stock." When you're selecting a new vehicle, give as much priority to its fuel efficiency and pollution potential as you do its utility. This saves money in the long run on fuel, maintenance, inspections, and carbon taxes (the new wave in pollution control, now appearing in Europe and certain to take effect soon across the Atlantic).

Keep mile-per-gallon records for your current vehicles to get a perspective on your fuel use, and always keep your vehicles tuned. A tuned vehicle with a clean fuel filter uses nine percent less gas than one without. Also inflate your tires. Fully-inflated tires reduce rolling resistance, which can boost your gas mileage five percent over flatter tires. And never leave a gas or light-diesel engine idling for more than 60 seconds.

The basic requisite for all maintenance on your vehicles is a log book, where you keep records of trips, tune-ups, oil/lube, gas purchases, mileage, etc. This also is your record of receipts and business vehicle use for tax computations. Use the American Camping Association's *Vehicle Log* to record tune-ups and gas mileage.

If any of your vehicles has an air conditioner, take it in to check for system leaks that may be emitting CFCs into the atmosphere. If the system cannot be repaired, you may have to have it pulled and replaced.

As a general policy, have each driver of any vehicle check its tire inflation, fluid levels, current license tabs, insurance receipt and registration, lights, turn signals, wipers, horn, and brakes before driving away. The laws of every state place responsibility for the car on its driver, not its owner.

FINAL THOUGHTS

Energy efficiency can be as simple as turning off an electric stove burner before the food is completely cooked or as complex as installing a solar heating system throughout all the buildings in your camp. But ultimately, no matter how little or much you spend on the initial program, energy-saving methods save substantial dollars in the long term. Your contribution to the Earth's future has an even longer impact.

WORKSHEET 6–1
ELECTRIC ENERGY USE

Use this worksheet to determine yearly, seasonal, and monthly usage trends and costs. Compare this year's worksheet to each of the following years' worksheets once you take appropriate energy-saving steps. Billing is usually in kilowatt hours (kwh) or 1,000 watt hours of use.

DATE _____

MONTH	KWH	×	RATE	=	TOTAL CHARGE
January	_____		_____		_____
February	_____		_____		_____
March	_____		_____		_____
April	_____		_____		_____
May	_____		_____		_____
June	_____		_____		_____
July	_____		_____		_____
August	_____		_____		_____
September	_____		_____		_____
October	_____		_____		_____
November	_____		_____		_____
December	_____		_____		_____
Total	_____		_____		_____

Average kwh per month (divide total kwh by 12)   _____ kwh

Average cost per month (divide total charge by 12) $ _____

Percentage of total electricity used for lighting (from Worksheet 6-4) _____ percent.

WORKSHEET 6-2
NATURAL GAS ENERGY USE

Use this worksheet to figure yearly, seasonal, and monthly usage trends and costs. Compare this year's worksheet to each of the following years' worksheets once you take appropriate energy-saving steps. Billing is usually in cubic feet (CF) or therms (TH).

DATE _____

MONTH	CF OR TH	×	RATE	=	TOTAL CHARGE
January	_____		_____		_____
February	_____		_____		_____
March	_____		_____		_____
April	_____		_____		_____
May	_____		_____		_____
June	_____		_____		_____
July	_____		_____		_____
August	_____		_____		_____
September	_____		_____		_____
October	_____		_____		_____
November	_____		_____		_____
December	_____		_____		_____
Total	_____		_____		_____

Average CF used per month (divide total CF by 12) _____ CF

Average cost per month (divide total charge by 12) $ _____

WORKSHEET 6-3
OIL ENERGY USE

Use this worksheet to determine yearly, seasonal, and monthly usage trends and costs. Compare this year's worksheet to each of the following years' worksheets once you take appropriate energy-saving steps. Billing is usually in gallons.

DATE _____

MONTH	GALLONS	×	RATE	=	TOTAL CHARGE
January	_____		_____		_____
February	_____		_____		_____
March	_____		_____		_____
April	_____		_____		_____
May	_____		_____		_____
June	_____		_____		_____
July	_____		_____		_____
August	_____		_____		_____
September	_____		_____		_____
October	_____		_____		_____
November	_____		_____		_____
December	_____		_____		_____
Total	_____		_____		_____

Average gallons used per month (divide total gallons by 12)
_____ gallons

Average cost per month (divide total charge by 12) $ _____

WORKSHEET 6–4
LIGHTING INVENTORY

Use this worksheet to determine how much of your energy is used to light your facility. Indicate building name or other location of lighting, type of lighting, wattage, number of lamps, and use per day. Use the following letters to indicate type of lighting:

F = fluorescent (check ballasts, not lamps)

I = incandescent

H = halogen

S = sodium vapor

HL = halide

LOCATION	LIGHTING TYPE	WATTAGE	×	NUMBER OF LAMPS	×	HOURS USED PER DAY	=	TOTAL WATT HOURS PER DAY
_____	_____	_____		_____		_____		_____
_____	_____	_____		_____		_____		_____
_____	_____	_____		_____		_____		_____
_____	_____	_____		_____		_____		_____
_____	_____	_____		_____		_____		_____
_____	_____	_____		_____		_____		_____
_____	_____	_____		_____		_____		_____
_____	_____	_____		_____		_____		_____
_____	_____	_____		_____		_____		_____
_____	_____	_____		_____		_____		_____
_____	_____	_____		_____		_____		_____
_____	_____	_____		_____		_____		_____
_____	_____	_____		_____		_____		_____
_____	_____	_____		_____		_____		_____
_____	_____	_____		_____		_____		_____
_____	_____	_____		_____		_____		_____
_____	_____	_____		_____		_____		_____
Total	_____	_____		_____		_____		_____

Total kwh per day (divide total watt hours per day by 1,000) _____ kwh

Total kwh per month (multiply kwh by days per month) _____ kwh

Percentage of total electric used for lighting

(total lighting kwh ÷ total kwh from electric bill) = _____ percent

WORKSHEET 6–5
WATER HEATERS

Use this worksheet to track the steps your camp takes to make water heaters more efficient. Remember, every 10 degrees you set back the temperature can reduce your water heating energy by up to 6 percent.

Heater Location: <u>kitchen</u> Purpose: <u>dishwashing</u>

Type _____ gas _____ electric

Current temperature setting _____ F

Set to 130 to 140˚F _____ Y _____ N

Degree change _____ ÷ 10˚F × 6% ≅ percent energy saved _____

Wrapped in insulator jacket? _____ Y _____ N

Hot water pipes wrapped? _____ Y _____ N

Sediment flushed _____ Y _____ N _____ Date

Heater Location _____ Purpose _____

Type _____ gas _____ electric

Current temperature setting _____ F

Set back to 110˚F _____ Y _____ N

Degree change _____ ÷ 10˚F × 6% ≅ percent energy saved _____

Wrapped in insulator jacket? _____ Y _____ N

Hot water pipes wrapped? _____ Y _____ N

Sediment flushed _____ Y _____ N _____ Date

Heater Location _____ Purpose _____

Type _____ gas _____ electric

Current temperature setting _____ F

Set back to 110˚F _____ Y _____ N

Degree change _____ ÷ 10˚F × 6% ≅ percent energy saved _____

Wrapped in insulator jacket? _____ Y _____ N

Hot water pipes wrapped? _____ Y _____ N

Sediment flushed _____ Y _____ N _____ Date

Heater Location _____ Purpose _____

Type _____ gas _____ electric

Current temperature setting _____ F

Set back to 110°F _____ Y _____ N

Degree change _____ ÷ 10°F × 6% ≅ percent energy saved _____

Wrapped in insulator jacket? _____ Y _____ N

Hot water pipes wrapped? _____ Y _____ N

Sediment flushed _____ Y _____ N _____ Date

Heater Location _____ Purpose _____

Type _____ gas _____ electric

Current temperature setting _____ F

Set back to 110°F _____ Y _____ N

Degree change _____ ÷ 10°F × 6% ≅ percent energy saved _____

Wrapped in insulator jacket? _____ Y _____ N

Hot water pipes wrapped? _____ Y _____ N

Sediment flushed _____ Y _____ N _____ Date

Heater Location _____ Purpose _____

Type _____ gas _____ electric

Current temperature setting _____ F

Set back to 110°F _____ Y _____ N

Degree change _____ ÷ 10°F × 6% ≅ percent energy saved _____

Wrapped in insulator jacket? _____ Y _____ N

Hot water pipes wrapped? _____ Y _____ N

Sediment flushed _____ Y _____ N _____ Date

Heater Location _____ Purpose _____

Type _____ gas _____ electric

Current temperature setting _____ F

Set back to 110°F _____ Y _____ N

Degree change _____ ÷ 10°F × 6% ≅ percent energy saved _____

Wrapped in insulator jacket? _____ Y _____ N

Hot water pipes wrapped? _____ Y _____ N

Sediment flushed _____ Y _____ N _____ Date

WORKSHEET 6-6
SPACE HEATER MAINTENANCE

Use this worksheet to track regular maintenance on heaters. Use one worksheet per heater.

Building _____

Heat type _____ forced air _____ baseboard

_____ radiant _____ steam

Energy source _____ electric _____ gas _____ oil

Heat pump _____ Y _____ N

Thermostat type _____ manual _____ automatic

Thermostat day setting _____ F

Thermostat night setting _____ F

Heater checked? _____ date _____ initials

Repair/replace? Parts? _____

By whom? _____

Company _____

Address _____

Phone _____

Heat pump checked? _____ date _____ initials

Repair/replace? Parts? _____

By whom? _____

Company _____

Address _____

Phone _____

Machinery cleaned, lubricated? _____ date _____ initials

Repair/replace? Parts? _____

By whom? _____

Company _____

Address _____

Phone _____

Filters cleaned? _____ date _____ initials

Filters replaced? _____ date _____ initials

Ductwork cleaned? _____ date _____ initials

WORKSHEET 6-7
SPACE HEATER AUDIT

Use this worksheet to begin your audit when considering heater upgrades. Use one per heater.

Building _____

Heat type _____ forced air _____ baseboard

_____ radiant _____ steam

Energy source _____ electric _____ gas _____ oil

Heat pump _____ Y _____ N

Thermostat type _____ manual _____ automatic

Thermostat day setting _____ F

Thermostat night setting _____ F

Ducts insulated _____ Y _____ N

Efficiency audit performed _____ Y _____ N _____ date

Auditor _____

Company _____

Address _____

Phone _____

More efficient fuel or energy source available _____ Y _____ N

Type _____ Cost _____ Payback period _____

Type _____ Cost _____ Payback period _____

More efficient heater available _____ Y _____ N

Type _____ Cost _____ Payback period _____

Type _____ Cost _____ Payback period _____

Replace with more efficient system _____ Y _____ N

Replace manual thermostat with automatic _____ Y _____ N

Other efficiency options:

Recaulk window and door frames _____ Y _____ N

Add storm windows _____ Y _____ N

Replace windows and doors _____ Y _____ N

Add ceiling fan _____ Y _____ N

Add insulation _____ ceiling _____ floor _____ walls

_____ north wall only

Add awnings _____ Y _____ N

Plant deciduous trees on south side _____ Y _____ N

WORKSHEET 6–8
AIR CONDITIONER MAINTENANCE

Use this worksheet to track regular maintenance on air conditioners. Use one worksheet per air conditioning unit.

Building _____

Air conditioning type _____ window mount _____ central

Energy source _____ electric _____ natural gas

Thermostat type _____ manual _____ automatic

Thermostat day setting _____ F

Thermostat night setting _____ F

Air conditioner checked? _____ date _____ initials

Repair/replace? Parts? _____

By whom? _____

Company _____

Address _____

Phone _____

Machinery cleaned, lubricated? _____ date _____ initials

Repair/replace? Parts? _____

By whom? _____

Company _____

Address _____

Phone _____

Filter cleaned? _____ date _____ initials

Filter replaced? _____ date _____ initials

Ductwork cleaned? _____ date _____ initials

WORKSHEET 6-9
AIR CONDITIONER AUDIT

Use this worksheet to begin your audit when considering air conditioner upgrades. Use one per air conditioning unit.

Building _____

Air conditioning type _____ window mount _____ central

Energy source _____ electric _____ natural gas

Thermostat type _____ manual _____ automatic

Thermostat day setting _____ F

Thermostat night setting _____ F

Ducts insulated _____ Y _____ N

Efficiency audit performed _____ Y _____ N _____ date

Auditor _____

Company _____

Address _____

Phone _____

More efficient energy source available _____ Y _____ N

Type _____ Cost _____ Payback period _____

Type _____ Cost _____ Payback period _____

More efficient alternative _____ Y _____ N

Type _____ Cost _____ Payback period _____

Type _____ Cost _____ Payback period _____

Replace with more efficient unit _____ Y _____ N

Other efficiency options:

Replace with ceiling or other ventilation fans _____ Y _____ N

Recaulk window and door frames _____ Y _____ N

Add storm windows _____ Y _____ N

Replace windows and doors _____ Y _____ N

Add ceiling fan _____ Y _____ N

Add insulation _____ ceiling _____ floor _____ walls

_____ north wall only

Add awnings _____ Y _____ N

Plant deciduous trees on south side _____ Y _____ N

WORKSHEET 6–10
ELECTRIC EQUIPMENT

Use this worksheet to track regular maintenance on electric equipment.

LOCATION	SERVICED	DATE
Compressors		
_____	Y _____ N _____	_____
_____	Y _____ N _____	_____
_____	Y _____ N _____	_____
_____	Y _____ N _____	_____
Refrigerated drinking fountains		
_____	Y _____ N _____	_____
_____	Y _____ N _____	_____
_____	Y _____ N _____	_____
_____	Y _____ N _____	_____
Kitchen mixers		
_____	Y _____ N _____	_____
_____	Y _____ N _____	_____
_____	Y _____ N _____	_____
_____	Y _____ N _____	_____
Kitchen slicers		
_____	Y _____ N _____	_____
_____	Y _____ N _____	_____
_____	Y _____ N _____	_____
_____	Y _____ N _____	_____
Fans (windows and exhaust)		
_____	Y _____ N _____	_____
_____	Y _____ N _____	_____
_____	Y _____ N _____	_____
_____	Y _____ N _____	_____
Electric tools		
_____	Y _____ N _____	_____
_____	Y _____ N _____	_____
_____	Y _____ N _____	_____
_____	Y _____ N _____	_____

Generators

_____	Y _____ N _____	_____
_____	Y _____ N _____	_____
_____	Y _____ N _____	_____
_____	Y _____ N _____	_____

Air conditioning units

_____	Y _____ N _____	_____
_____	Y _____ N _____	_____
_____	Y _____ N _____	_____
_____	Y _____ N _____	_____

Heaters

_____	Y _____ N _____	_____
_____	Y _____ N _____	_____
_____	Y _____ N _____	_____
_____	Y _____ N _____	_____

Refrigerators/freezers

_____	Y _____ N _____	_____
_____	Y _____ N _____	_____
_____	Y _____ N _____	_____
_____	Y _____ N _____	_____

Ovens/stoves

_____	Y _____ N _____	_____
_____	Y _____ N _____	_____
_____	Y _____ N _____	_____
_____	Y _____ N _____	_____

Other

_____	Y _____ N _____	_____
_____	Y _____ N _____	_____
_____	Y _____ N _____	_____
_____	Y _____ N _____	_____
_____	Y _____ N _____	_____
_____	Y _____ N _____	_____
_____	Y _____ N _____	_____
_____	Y _____ N _____	_____
	Y _____ N _____	_____

WORKSHEET 6-11
BUILDING INSULATION

Use this worksheet to list existing building insulation or plan insulation upgrades.

BUILDING	INSULATE	WALL	TYPE FLOOR	CEIL-ING
Cabin 1	Y _____ N _____	_____	_____	_____
Cabin 2	Y _____ N _____	_____	_____	_____
Cabin 3	Y _____ N _____	_____	_____	_____
Cabin 4	Y _____ N _____	_____	_____	_____
Cabin 5	Y _____ N _____	_____	_____	_____
Cabin 6	Y _____ N _____	_____	_____	_____
Cabin 7	Y _____ N _____	_____	_____	_____
Administration building	Y _____ N _____	_____	_____	_____
Dining hall	Y _____ N _____	_____	_____	_____
Staff housing	Y _____ N _____	_____	_____	_____
Health center	Y _____ N _____	_____	_____	_____
Activities building	Y _____ N _____	_____	_____	_____
_____	Y _____ N _____	_____	_____	_____
_____	Y _____ N _____	_____	_____	_____
_____	Y _____ N _____	_____	_____	_____
_____	Y _____ N _____	_____	_____	_____
_____	Y _____ N _____	_____	_____	_____
_____	Y _____ N _____	_____	_____	_____
_____	Y _____ N _____	_____	_____	_____
_____	Y _____ N _____	_____	_____	_____
_____	Y _____ N _____	_____	_____	_____
_____	Y _____ N _____	_____	_____	_____
_____	Y _____ N _____	_____	_____	_____
_____	Y _____ N _____	_____	_____	_____
_____	Y _____ N _____	_____	_____	_____
_____	Y _____ N _____	_____	_____	_____
_____	Y _____ N _____	_____	_____	_____
_____	Y _____ N _____	_____	_____	_____
_____	Y _____ N _____	_____	_____	_____

WORKSHEET 6–12
VEHICLE INFORMATION SHEET

Use this worksheet each time any maintenance or maintenance checks are completed on any vehicle. Use one per vehicle per service.

Date _____ .

Vehicle _____

License plate _____

Purchase date _____

Mileage at purchase _____ Current mileage _____

Fuel type _____ Miles/gallon _____

Plates current? _____ Y _____ N Renewal date _____

Insurance current _____ Y _____ N Renewal date _____

Last emissions test date _____

Results:

Hydrocarbons (HC) _____

Carbon monoxide (CO) _____

Carbon dioxide (CO_2) _____

Last tune-up date _____ Miles _____

Last oil change/lube date _____ Miles _____

Preventive maintenance check _____ Date _____ Initials

Fluid levels:

Windshield _____ OK _____ add

Brake _____ OK _____ add

Transmission _____ OK _____ add

Turn signals _____ OK _____ repair _____ L _____ R

Headlights _____ OK _____ repair _____ LF _____ RF

_____ LR _____ RR

Brake lights _____ OK _____ repair _____ L _____ R

Wipers _____ OK _____ repair _____ L _____ R

Oil

Level _____ OK _____ low

Quarts added _____ Oil weight _____

Oil filter changed _____ Y _____ N

Fuel filter changed _____ Y _____ N

Radiator

Fluid level _____ OK _____ low

Hoses OK _____ Y _____ N Replaced _____ Y _____ N

Leaks _____ Y _____ N Where _____

Taken for repair _____ Y _____ N

Winterized _____ Y _____ N

Battery installed _____ Warranty life _____ years

Condition _____ OK _____ problem: _____

Repair/replacement _____ Y _____ N

Spark plugs checked _____ Y _____ N

Cleaned and gapped _____ Replaced _____

Air conditioner _____ OK _____ problem: _____

Repair/replacement _____ Y _____ N

Horn _____ OK _____ repair

Air filter changed _____ Y _____ N

TIRES	CONDITION	OK	PSI	REPLACE	DATE
Front right	_____	_____	_____	_____	_____
Front left	_____	_____	_____	_____	_____
Back right	_____	_____	_____	_____	_____
Back left	_____	_____	_____	_____	_____
For vehicles with more than four wheels:					
Back right #2	_____	_____	_____	_____	_____
Back right #3	_____	_____	_____	_____	_____
Back right #4	_____	_____	_____	_____	_____
Back left #2	_____	_____	_____	_____	_____
Back left #3	_____	_____	_____	_____	_____
Back left #4	_____	_____	_____	_____	_____

7

PRECYCLING SUPPLIES AND SUPPLIERS

"Garbage in, garbage out."
—Computer litany

The simple litany at the beginning of this chapter is the philosophy behind precycling, or reducing the amount of material you import into your camp. The more you bring in, the more you potentially throw out. Fortunately, this also works with less—the less you import, the less you export.

The camp kitchens at Brandeis-Bardin Institute (BBI) generated approximately 85 percent of the two camps' trash. Of that, almost half was food waste we could compost, a quarter was recyclables, such as cardboard, glass, aluminum, steel, plastic, and paper, and a quarter was throw-aways, such as non-recyclable plastics, multi-layer packages, broken dishes, batteries, etc. By precycling, the camp reduced its trash output by 10 to 20 percent. At BBI, that equaled about three dumpsters or roughly nine tons over the 10–week span.

According to the latest EPA figures (1990), Americans produce about 196 million tons of solid waste a year; over 37 percent is paper products, about 25 percent is food and yard waste, and about 15 percent is metals and glass. The 20 to 25 percent that remains is plastics, wood, and organics, such as leather, mattresses, construction debris, etc.

Today, landfills are closing, and a growing number of states (33 as of

A Closer Look

The EPA estimates that up to 80 percent of what we currently throw away can be reclaimed.

1992) prohibit citizens from throwing out yard clippings with the garbage. More municipalities are starting recycling programs and large-scale yard waste composting, several have pilot programs for food waste collection, and more than 160 are capturing methane generated from decomposing landfills to power electric generators and machinery. The trend on the local level is to write commercial building codes to require that remodeling and new construction designs include space for storing recyclable and compostable materials.

In the future, camps may likely be required to separate everything we once just threw out into neat piles for collection: aluminum, steel, plastics (more than seven types), glass, paper, cardboard, food, and yard debris. In short, there's no longer any such thing as garbage.

Finding the storage space for this activity and creating or buying storage bins can be difficult and expensive. The time that separation activities consume, and the costs in direct labor and program time will also impact the bottom line still further. But, how do you defend yourself and your camp against these eventualities? By precycling.

Precycling is simply minimizing the amount of trash your camp outputs by controlling the products you input. This "source reduction" enables you to increase your ordering efficiency and reduce costs for purchasing, trash separating, and hauling. (It also sets a good example for participants and their parents.)

GOOD BUYS AND GOOD-BYES

For precycling, keep two questions in mind:

1. "Does our camp need this?"
2. "Does our camp need this many?"

And in both cases, buy only what is necessary.

For example, most of what you buy for your food service program comes in recyclable packages. For instance, foods, oils, and drinks come in plastic, glass, steel, and aluminum containers, packed in paper or cardboard cases. Flour comes in heavy paper bags, baking soda in paper boxes. Nearly all can be recycled, so these are good buys.

But the problem in many cases begins with shrink-wrapped packaging. Where do you dispose of the plastic films? The garbage can. Next, many food service-size condiments, such as mustard and mayonnaise, come in large plastic containers, some of which cannot be recycled. Although camps could use these jars to store other items in art rooms, shops, and offices, most food-service operations simply toss them.

Other food items commonly thrown out at camps are

❑ Brick-pack juice boxes, single serve (250 ml/8.45 ounce) and larger, made of layered cardboard, foil, and plastic. These are rarely reusable nor recyclable.

❑ Frozen juice containers, either a box of layered cardboard and plastic or a layered tube with tin ends. Some can be reused for craft projects.

❏ Single-serve plastic and foil condiment packs. These are generally not reusable or recyclable.

❏ Single-serve plastic and foil pudding and yogurt tubs. Some can be reused in crafts and other projects, but they are generally not recyclable.

❏ Plastic six-pack rings. If you're creative, these can be used in craft projects, but they are not recyclable.

❏ Plastic dishes and utensils, disposable aprons and gloves, and other plastic materials. These generally are not reusable or recyclable.

The kitchens at BBI, which served 1,500 meals a day, threw out 5 pounds of plastic items a day—a total of nearly 500 pounds for the camp season. Multiply only half that output by the number of camps in North America, and the result is several hundred thousand pounds of plastics camps dump nationwide in just one summer.

REDUCE

Examine all the packaging for items you buy, whether plastics, paper, aluminum, steel, or glass. By reducing the quantity you buy, you save money up front and cut your trash output by up to 20 percent. As you review your order list, refer to Worksheet 7–1: Purchasing Possibilities at the end of this chapter.

It's also a good idea to indicate on files or rolodex cards the vendors who will work with you on precycling issues and offer suggestions toward this goal.

SINGLE SERVE VS. BULK

A Closer Look

Again, you have to weigh the advantages and disadvantages of each single-serve vs. bulk product, always considering the broader environmental costs.

Single-serve packages can be wasteful because they require so much packaging as a matter of course. Bulk-pack food stuffs can minimize packaging waste but may create greater food waste. You need to weigh the packaging waste against the food waste for each food item at your camp and buy appropriately.

For example, the BBI camps found that table pitchers for syrup, filled from bulk packs, were spilled, became crusty, and needed cleaning often. Filling them was also messy. And on picnics, it was healthier to have single-serve packs of mayonnaise than an open jar sitting in the sun. In both situations, the camps wasted a great deal by buying in bulk.

On the other hand, single-serve packs of cereal often prove to be wasteful. The family-sized boxes get used up before they go stale and aren't particularly messy, so there is no need to add the extra packaging of single-serve cereal boxes.

Milk in 6–gallon containers is often more expensive than in 1–gallon jugs, and the gallon jugs are reusable, made of recyclable high-density polyethylene (HDPE), and don't require an investment in a refrigerated serving box or pitchers that must be handled, washed, and stored. If you are not taking milk on a picnic and therefore don't need a single-serve package, you might opt for the gallon size jugs as opposed to the institutional size ones.

DISHWARE

If you use disposable dishware and flatware, consider replacing them with permanent ware. For a camp that serves 1,500 meals a day, the cost for disposables can run over $15,000 per 10–week season. Permanent ware represents a one-time investment; it also avoids further costs for disposing the paper and plastic utensils. However, if your camp changes to permanent dishware, plan for new dining hall logistics of collecting, scraping, and washing the utensils. This will take more time than throwing out the disposables!

Potential Pitfalls

Remember to introduce precycling gradually: Saving the world is urgent, but people's habits take time to change. Press on too quickly and they resist, even if they know they are resisting good ideas.

If your camp already uses permanent dishware, get in the habit of taking it on picnics, too. If you must carry disposables on picnics, it's ecologically best to bring paper products for dishware and napkins, and permanent metal flatware. Since plastic flatware cannot be recycled at this time, if you use it, collect the pieces after the picnic, run them through the camp dishwasher to clean off the food waste, and reuse.

As for paper dishes and bowls, use non-coated, chemical free, recycled fiber varieties. Even dirtied with food waste, these can be used as bedding for compost (see Chapter 8). Again, work with your restaurant supply vendors as well as other product vendors, and with your staff on this project.

Overall, experiment to find the alternatives that are most environmentally sound, healthy, and cost-effective for you. Hopefully, each option you choose will be all three.

FINAL THOUGHTS

Precycling can be one of the more effortless and quickest ways to cut down on solid waste disposal at your camp. It's not, however, a decision you can implement across the board—sometimes what appears to be wasted packaging is a smarter environmental (and financial) buy than an industrial-size portion of that item. Be sure to weigh your choices on a case-by-case basis.

WORKSHEET 7-1
PURCHASING POSSIBILITIES

Can we buy items packaged in recyclable materials? _____ Y _____ N

Which ones? _____

From which vendors? _____

Can we buy any supplies in bigger/bulk sizes? _____ Y _____ N

Which ones? _____

From which vendors? _____

Can we eliminate single-serve in favor of larger units? _____ Y _____ N

Find single-serve units in recyclable packages? _____ Y _____ N

Which ones? _____

From which vendors? _____

Can we eliminate items that generate large amounts of waste?

_____ Y _____ N

Which ones? _____

From which vendors? _____

Can we eliminate junk mailings? _____ Y _____ N

Which ones? _____

From which vendors? _____

Can we cut down on disposable materials, such as throw-away plastic
aprons, gloves, dishware, tablecovers, in favor of permanent items?

_____ Y _____ N

Which ones? _____

From which vendors? _____

Can we buy durable, reusable products, such as refillable containers,
heavy-duty tarps, towels, etc.? _____ Y _____ N

Suggestions: _____

Can we reuse/repair office equipment, clothing, sports equipment?
_____ Y _____ N

Which ones? _____

Can we redirect "wastes" such as landscape trimmings and food
scraps for compost? _____ Y _____ N

Suggestions: _____

Can we eliminate or reuse solvents, lubricants, and other vehicle,
machinery, and maintenance items? _____ Y _____ N

Which ones? _____

Alternatives _____

Vendors _____

8

RECYCLING

"It is obvious, from the law of conservation of matter, that waste is produced in exactly the amount that resources are produced. What is not so obvious is that, in the long run, the reverse is also true: resource production depends upon the utilization of waste."

—René Dubos, ecologist, author ("The Global Dump Heap")

The previous chapter gave some background on precycling to cut down on solid waste output. This chapter addresses how to reduce your waste output further through recycling efforts. Recycling can reduce your trash output by as much as 50 percent, and, therefore, cut your trash hauling costs by half, too. It is also an opportunity to teach valuable, hands-on lessons to everyone at camp. Once you start recycling, you will find that nearly everything is potentially recyclable.

THE KITCHEN, YOUR LARGEST SOURCE

The BBI camps generated most of their recyclable materials in the kitchens. Odds are good that your camp is the same. Collectable items in this area include cardboard and paperboard boxes, steel and aluminum cans and foils, glass jars, and plastic milk, juice and condiment jugs and jars.

The BBI kitchens, which serve 1,500 meals a day (three meals a day for 350, plus afternoon and evening snacks), collected 500 pounds of cardboard, 230 pounds of steel, and 35 pounds each of aluminum, glass, and plastic every week. Over the 10-week camp season, this quantity tallied to more than four tons of material, enough to fill a 40-yard dumpster twice. Coupled with the more than 2 tons of food waste a week that was

A Closer Look

Generally, the camp kitchen produces the most waste material, with the administration office, maintenance building, and arts and craft area following behind. Concentrate recycling efforts in these areas.

A Closer Look

Law of conservation of matter: Mass-energy may not be created or destroyed, but each may be converted into each other.

removed for composting, and a shift from disposable to permanent flatware, BBI reduced its trash output from three dumpsters a week to one every 10 days. That alone saved more than $3,000 in trash hauling fees over the summer. Your savings will vary depending on your camp's output, and the fees your local hauler charges for dumpster rental and pickup.

The second most prolific recyclables source will probably be your administrative offices, which produce primarily paper from printers, copy machines, mail, and correspondence. Other recycling sources include your maintenance department, which generates boxes, paper, and scrap metals; your staff and campers, who generate aluminum and glass beverage containers, boxes, magazines, correspondence, and newsprint; and your art rooms, which may be able to both generate recyclable materials and use non-recyclables for art projects.

In the bigger picture, these recycling efforts also reduce the amounts of raw materials, energy, and water that manufacturers need to produce new paper products, metals, glass, and plastics, and it reduces the amount of pollution they generate. The composted material can become a soil additive or mulch for your garden beds, which reduces your costs for replacement topsoil, for watering, and for weed and pest killers.

Since the kitchen produces most of your waste material, this should be the focal point to begin your recycling. First, you need to study your existing situation, then calculate your recyclable materials output, talk to local recyclers, and decide which material(s) you will recycle and how. Finally, designate a supervisor for the project, and enlist everyone's support. Worksheet 8-1 at the end of this chapter can guide you through the process.

CALCULATING MATERIALS OUTPUT

There are at least two ways to calculate your output. The first is to assume a quantity using Worksheet 8-2: "Ballpark" Estimate of Waste at the end of this chapter. Using this method, you can estimate waste output and therefore possible recyclables without having to review your purchasing and inventory lists item by item.

A more specific way to calculate quantities is to use Worksheet 8-3: Average Material Output.

NOTES ABOUT PLASTICS

The National Association for Plastic Container Recovery (NAPCOR) and other industry spokespeople make a number of assertions about plastics:

❏ Plastics have great utility.

❏ Disposables are cheaper than their paper and metal competitors.

❏ All plastic can be recycled.

❏ Plastics account for a relatively small proportion of America's solid waste.

❏ Disposables are more ecological than permanent ware because they take less energy to produce, and they don't need to be washed, which requires precious water and energy and uses polluting detergents.

A Closer Look

Currently, there are seven major types of consumer plastics on the market:

 PET (polyethylene teraphthalate): one- and two-liter soda bottles, some food, sauce and sundries packages.

 HDPE (high-density polyethylene): gallon milk and juice jugs, some food packages.

 PVC (polyvinyl chloride): food and mineral water bottles.

 LDPE (low-density polyethylene): some food product containers and lids, and plastic grocery and shopping bags.

 PP (polypropylene): medical cases, cereal box liners.

 PS (polystyrene): cookie, muffin and deli trays, and fast-food cutlery. (Styrofoam cups and egg cartons are also #6, but they are EPS—expanded polystyrene).

 Other (multiple plastic resins): layered products, such as potato and corn chip bags and some deli trays.

Environmentalists' reply:

❏ Plastic wares have utility, but in the long run, they are more expensive than permanent ware as they are made of non-renewable petroleum. They also are a major contributor to solid waste (7 to 9 percent of our annual 180 million tons, and 20 percent of landfill volume, according to the EPA).

❏ As of 1990, the plastics industry was recycling less than one percent of the 62 billion pounds of plastics it produces every year (*Resource Recycling*, 4/91). Of that total, about half, or 25 to 30 billion pounds, is disposables. The industry has pledged (and some states have mandated) to achieve a 25 percent recycling rate for some plastics by 1995, but even if it meets that optimistic projection, 80 percent of available plastics will still be thrown away, and *more* plastics will probably be in use.

❏ Environmentalists take less issue with durable, reusable plastic ware than with disposables, although the durables require water, energy, and soaps to clean.

The plastics industry is making recycling progress. It is committed to recycling 25 percent of certain types by 1995, and PET soda bottles have surpassed that already. It is increasingly identifying its wares by type with numbered triangles to facilitate collection and sorting (see sidebar). It's experimenting with new, non-petroleum, biodegradable materials as bases for plastic resins. And new recycling technologies are being developed, most notably an atomizer system that separates mixed plastics by molecular structure. But, all these advances are still some years from commercial availability.

Currently, only three types of plastic are widely recycled in the U.S.: 1 PET, 2 HDPE, and 4 LDPE. In 1992, of 23,000 communities in the U.S., less than 2,000 collected "at least one type of plastic," according to NAPCOR. That type is mostly 1 PET soda bottles. Many towns also collect 2 HDPE and 3 PVC milk and juice jugs, and some even collect 4 LDPE shopping bags.

A dismaying twist to plastics recycling is that there are subgroups of plastics within each of the seven types listed in the sidebar. This means that items in the same class of plastic, such as HDPE, may be formulated with different resins and need different solvents to break them down for reprocessing, so they must be further separated to be recycled.

For consumers then, simply separating these seven plastics according to their package markings isn't enough to guarantee their recycling. Who will take responsibility for the additional separations? The consumer, the waste hauler, or the recycler?

In the future, food and consumer product companies may narrow their plastic packaging materials to the most recyclable types—PET 1, HDPE 2, and LDPE 4—formulated with one type of resin, to facilitate better waste collection and recycling.

But, practically speaking, for the next five years, your camp will throw out most plastics, whether packaging disposable dishware and flatware, films, or containers. Thus, your best environmental bet is to concentrate on precycling and finding more environmentally friendly substitutes, even if they are permanent plastic items.

DECIDING WHICH MATERIAL TO RECYCLE

Once you calculate your materials output, you are ready to talk with local trash haulers and recyclers. By all means, call your current trash hauler, but also check in the *Yellow Pages* under "Recycling," "Waste Reduction," "Trash Removal," and "Rubbish Removal" to compare available services. Ask each hauler for a detailed list of which materials it recycles, and how it collects those materials.

Some trash haulers pick up your recyclable materials free, on the regular garbage pickup day. If haulers or recyclers in your area don't offer the free service, talk to them about the cost and frequency of collection.

Be aware that how you store recyclable materials can affect your costs. If a trash hauler or recycler picks up your materials, that company may supply you with special collection containers at no charge. If it charges, the larger the container, the more it costs to rent, but it also takes you longer to fill it so you're charged for fewer pickups. The smaller the container, the less the rent, but you may fill it faster and be charged for more pickups. You could decide to build your own containers, too.

Have your materials output calculations in hand so the recycler can help you estimate which size dumpster(s) and/or collection bin(s) you need. Once you have total weight and time period estimates for each recyclable material, ask your hauler or recycler how much space each quantity of material will occupy. Then, divide the total space requirement by the number of weeks it takes to accumulate that amount.

For example, if you generate 5,000 pounds of corrugated cardboard in 10 weeks, your hauler might say it takes 1,000 cubic feet of space to store that amount. Divide that 1,000 cubic feet by the 10 weeks of accumulation time to get your weekly space requirement (100 cubic feet per week). With the hauler, decide whether it would be more economical to have weekly pickup from that size container (which you could build, or the company could supply) or an end-of-season pickup from a 40-yard (1,080 cubic foot) dumpster. Do the same arithmetic for your metals, paper, glass, and other recyclables.

There are some recyclers that pay a small fee per pound or ton for your recyclable materials. However, most who pay this fee require delivery to their location, so you need to weigh the cost of delivery against this income. Often, you do not earn enough cash from this source to make it worth your delivery time. Use Worksheet 8-4: Commercial Recycler Information at the end of this chapter to assist you with your decisions.

By now you should have a handle on how much recycling will cost (and save) your camp, and how much space to devote to a collection area. With this information, you can decide which material(s) to recycle this year and which to add to the program in subsequent years.

EQUIPPING THE SITE FOR RECYCLING You need very little equipment for recycling. It's a straightforward process of collecting items at source points, gathering them in one central location, then hauling them away. However, your equipment list should include the following items:

A Closer Look

Note: When a recycler or hauler asks you the weekly "tonnage" your camp will produce, realize that most camps throw out pounds, not tons, of materials each week. That's why you should ask the hauler to deliver dumpsters you can spend all season filling.

❏ Recycling collection bins: Depending on which material(s) you decide to recycle, you might need a variety of collection bins at various places around camp. Tough, plastic bins are now available at most hardware and building supply stores in the country. There are also two- and three-compartment units that can contain several types of recyclable materials. You simply hang a heavy trash bag in each compartment, and remove it when it's full. Specialty companies, such as Toter® and Rubbermaid®, make 15- to 90-gallon containers for collecting large quantities of materials. There are wheeled carts with up to 250-gallon capacities, too, which may be good for the central collection location.

The best collection solution in kitchens, which tend to be cramped, high-traffic areas, may be to use stackable bins, rather than grouping several bins together. If bins fill quickly, add others as needed, or dump the filled bins regularly in an outdoor collection area.

Be sure that the collection bins for each material are marked clearly, or are different shapes or colors so it is obvious where to put aluminum, steel, glass, and different types of plastics, etc.

❏ Can openers: If you decide to recycle metals, you'll save yourself a lot of storage space by using a heavy-duty can opener to remove both ends of a can before you flatten it. Also use a can opener to take the ends off frozen juice containers that are made of paper sleeves.

❏ Aluminum can crushers: There are crushers available that are designed to be mounted on a wall. You can also go the old-fashioned route and crush cans by stepping on them. (This latter method can be enormous fun but should be well supervised if children are involved.)

You may want to set a policy on who may use can openers and crushers, then train these designated people to avoid damaged tools and liability with the users.

❏ Gloves: Heavy linen or leather gloves are the best protection for handling bins of collected aluminum and glass.

❏ Vehicle: You may want to designate a camp vehicle to carry collected materials to the central storage area, or if necessary, out of camp to the recycling center.

DESIGNATING SPACE FOR COLLECTION You must gather the recyclables you collect from different buildings and areas at a central location before they go to a recycler. You'll need a staging area of approximately 400 square feet (20 x 20) for this purpose. Any additional space you need depends on whether you have storage bins, dumpsters, or simply pile everything together.

Cardboard requires the most space, and boxes should be flattened to minimize the storage space requirement. As whole boxes, 500 pounds of cardboard can fill a room 10 feet wide, 10 feet long, and 8 feet high. That same room can hold roughly eight times, or 4,000 pounds, as much flattened cardboard. Most recyclers won't accept unflattened cardboard.

Potential Pitfall

In some "deposit states," soda cans must be left intact so recyclers can read the UPC codes for deposit reimbursement purposes. Ask your supplier if this rule applies to your camp.

A Closer Look

Collecting recyclables in containers rather than in piles always makes camp look cleaner and generally is a more efficient use of space.

A Closer Look

To save water when rinsing cans and bottles, fill a bucket and rinse the containers in it. When the water gets dirty, change it.

A Closer Look

If you expect your camp's overall environmental programs to become extensive, you may want to hire an environmental program advisor to help you design them, work out step-by-step plans, and train your staff and participants.

Cardboard boxes can be flattened and piled out on the loading dock by the kitchen staff as soon as they open them and remove their contents. From there, the boxes can be carried to the hauling-area bin or dumpster by hand or by vehicle.

It is much safer to store flattened aluminum in permanent containers or garbage cans, rather than heavy-duty trash bags. Likewise, glass *must* be stored in hard-sided containers, such as wood or heavy plastic boxes, metal trash cans, or steel drums to avoid spilling and injuries. Paper can be stored in cardboard boxes or shopping bags, and plastic can be collected in a kitchen bag-lined trash can and stored in trash bags.

When designating collection sites, your objective should be to find space for one staging area that can harbor all necessary collection bins and is as close to the usage areas as possible. Place the collection bins near a sink or dishwasher, where cans and bottles can be rinsed clean to eliminate their attraction to insects and rodents. Place can openers and crushers on the wall above the containers. Above all, be sure every recyclable storage area is clean and that containers are covered to deter rodents and avoid accidents.

DESIGNATING A SUPERVISOR Kitchen recycling tasks are generally part of the kitchen manager's job description. This person is responsible for seeing that recyclable and compostable materials are separated from garbage, transported to staging areas, and removed from camp.

The kitchen manager should be able to handle this extra project in addition to his or her other duties as long as your camp sets up an efficient recycling program. However, each step takes supervision, especially in the first weeks, so start your program by recycling only one item. Once the logistics and training for this activity are incorporated into the kitchen routine, you can add additional materials such as metal or glass containers for recycling. But, no matter whom you designate as supervisor, make it part of the job description and then be supportive, letting that person make suggestions, too.

FINAL THOUGHTS

Recycling has received a lot of publicity in today's growing environmental awareness. Because of this focus, the materials and advice you need to get started are at your fingertips. Just be sure to incorporate materials one at a time into your recycling program, and success is as close as the nearest garbage can!

WORKSHEET 8–1
A CHECKLIST

_____ 1. Calculate recyclable material output.

_____ 2. Talk to and make arrangements with a local recycler.

_____ 3. Decide which material(s) to recycle.

_____ 4. Make a plan of action for recycling.

_____ 5. Designate a recycling supervisor.

_____ 6. Enlist everyone's support.

_____ 7. Make a plan for integrating recycling into programming activities.

WORKSHEET 8-2
"BALLPARK" ESTIMATE OF WASTE

Every week, each person at camp generates the following amounts of waste on average. Multiply these amounts by the number of campers in your program per week to determine total materials output for each week.

Wasted food

8-11 pounds × number of campers _____ = total wasted food _____

Cardboard

1.4 pounds × number of campers _____ = total cardboard _____

Paper

0.4375 pounds × number of campers _____ = total paper _____

Steel

0.5625 pounds × number of campers _____ = total steel _____

Aluminum

0.125 pounds × number of campers _____ = total aluminum _____

Plastic

0.125 pounds × number of campers _____ = total plastic _____

Glass

0.125 pounds × number of campers _____ = total glass _____

WORKSHEET 8–3
AVERAGE MATERIAL OUTPUT

Use your purchase orders from last season as your guide when filling out this chart.

Glass

8-ounce jars: case of 24 = 9.4 pounds

9.4 pounds × number of cases ordered _____ = total weight _____

32-ounce jars: case of 12 = 12 pounds

12 pounds × number of cases ordered _____ = total weight _____

64-ounce jars: case of 6 = 8.9 pounds

8.9 pounds × number of cases ordered _____ = total weight _____

105-ounce jars: case of 4 = 10.2 pounds

10.2 pounds × number of cases ordered _____ = total weight _____

134-ounce jars: case of 4 = 10.75 pounds

10.75 pounds × number of cases ordered _____ = total weight _____

Long-neck soda bottles: case of 24 = 17 pounds

17 pounds × number of cases ordered _____ = total weight _____

12-ounce soda bottles: case of 24 = 10.5 pounds

10.5 pounds × number of cases ordered _____ = total weight _____

One-liter or quart bottles: case of 12 = 13.5 pounds

13.5 pounds × number of cases ordered _____ = total weight _____

Metals

Aluminum cans: case of 24 = 1 pound

1 pound × number of cases ordered _____ = total weight _____

Steel #10 cans: case of 6 = 3.5 pounds

3.5 pounds × number of cases ordered _____ = total weight _____

Cardboard

Average foodservice box = 1.3 pounds

1.3 pounds × number of boxes ordered _____ = total weight _____

Heavy tomato/fruit box = 2.5 pounds

2.5 pounds × number of cases ordered _____ = total weight _____

WORKSHEET 8–4
COMMERCIAL RECYCLER INFORMATION

Fill out this form for each recycler or trash hauler you contact. Compare notes on each and choose the best one for your camp's situation. Keep the information sheets in a file for later review.

Company name _____

Address _____

Address _____

Telephone _____

_____ Trash hauler

_____ City

_____ County

_____ Private recycler with pickup service

_____ Recycling drop-off center

This company recycles the following materials:

Paper

_____ Cardboard _____ Newsprint _____ Colored _____ Computer _____ Other
_____

_____ Mixed _____ Separated _____ Other _____

Metals

_____ Aluminum _____ Steel _____ Foils _____ Other _____

_____ Delabeled _____ Cleaned _____ Crushed _____ Other _____

Glass

_____ Green _____ Clear _____ Brown _____ Other _____

_____ With labels _____ Without labels _____ Rinsed _____ Whole _____ Mixed
_____ Other _____

Plastic

_____PET _____HDPE _____LDPE _____PE _____PS _____PP _____Other

_____ With labels _____ Without labels _____ Rinsed _____ Whole _____ Other

This company will pick up from us _____ Y _____ N

How often _____

This company requires the following special arrangements _____

_____

This company provides collection bins _____Y _____N

Size _____ Cost _____

Size _____ Cost _____

If we deliver, this company pays for our recyclables _____ Y _____ N

How much $ _____ per _____

WORKSHEET 8-5
WHAT AND WHERE TO RECYCLE

Use this form to record which recyclable materials you will collect from where.

Which materials will we recycle?

Paper

_____ Cardboard _____ Newsprint _____ Colored _____ Computer _____ Other

_____ Mixed _____ Separated _____ Other _____

Metals

_____ Aluminum _____ Steel _____ Foils _____ Other _____

_____ With labels _____ Without labels _____ Rinsed _____ Crushed _____
Other _____

Glass

_____ Green _____ Clear _____ Brown _____ Other _____

_____ With labels _____ Without labels _____ Rinsed _____ Whole _____ Mixed
_____ Other _____

Plastic

_____PET _____HDPE _____LDPE _____PE _____PS _____PP _____Other

_____ With labels _____ Without labels _____ Rinsed _____ Whole _____ Other

At which locations will we collect recyclables?

Kitchen

_____ Paper _____ Metals _____ Glass _____ Plastic

Office

_____ Paper _____ Metals _____ Glass _____ Plastic

Art room

_____ Paper _____ Metals _____ Glass _____ Plastic

155

Infirmary

_____ Paper _____ Metals _____ Glass _____ Plastic

Shop

_____ Paper _____ Metals _____ Glass _____ Plastic

Cabins

_____ Paper _____ Metals _____ Glass _____ Plastic

Other location _____

_____ Paper _____ Metals _____ Glass _____ Plastic

Other location _____

_____ Paper _____ Metals _____ Glass _____ Plastic

Where will we place the bins at each location?

_____ kitchen

_____ office

_____ art room

_____ activity room

_____ cabins

_____ dining hall

Who will flatten cardboard and cans; rinse and clean foil, cans, and bottles?

_____ Each individual at each location

_____ Staff member _____

_____ Other _____

Where will the central staging/hauling area be?

_____behind dining hall

_____ behind dumpsters

_____ other _____

How will we bring the recyclables from each location to the central storage area?

_____ Vehicle collection run

_____ Participants bring items to collection area

How often _____ Daily _____ Weekly

How often do we move the recyclables out of camp?

_____ Daily _____ Weekly _____ Monthly _____ Seasonally

Who will move recyclables? _____

WORKSHEET 8-6
DELEGATING DUTIES

Use this worksheet to delegate recycling responsibilities for a smooth operation.

Who will clean and prep the recyclable container(s) after each meal? _____ KP _____ Kitchen manager _____ Dishwasher _____ Campers

Who will flatten the cardboard boxes? _____ Staff/prep crew _____ KP _____ Kitchen manager _____ Campers

Who will haul the recyclables to the staging area? _____ Kitchen manager _____ Grounds crew

How do we intend to work the time it takes for recycling activities into our schedule? ___

_____

_____

_____

_____

Can we include participants in recycling efforts? _____ Y _____ N

Specifics: _____

_____

_____

_____

_____

How do we intend to include participants in recycling activities?

_____

_____

_____

_____

9
COMPOSTING

"Compost happens."
—bumper sticker, circa 1991

You may view food and paper scraps as garbage, but they are actually a double resource for your camp:

❏ A way to enrich your soil for plants and crops through composting, and
❏ A programming tool for illustrating growth cycles on Earth.

In 1990, BBI composted its camps' food scraps (excluding meat and dairy) with landscape clippings and hay to reduce its total trash output by approximately 20 percent. You may process far less material than this. Starting small takes a minimum of effort and materials, and enables you to control the process easily. Any amount you compost is that much less you put out for garbage.

You won't lack for raw materials, either: Generally, a camper who eats three square meals and snacks leaves 8 ounces to a pound of waste a day. If your kitchen serves 600 meals a day, you throw out 2,000 pounds of food scraps every week.

A Closer Look

Unlike recycling, composting can be done entirely inside camp, independent of the outside market forces that affect recycling. You can incorporate composting on any scale you choose, depending on your preferences and programming.

WHAT GOOD IS COMPOST?

Compost is an all-around, terrific soil additive. It's the end of the organic decomposition process: a dark, crumbly, earthy-smelling material, similar to potting soil. Next time you're deep in a forest, dig your hand down into the earth. See, feel, and smell the rich, dark soil. That's compost, made from forest plant material that has decomposed over many years.

Compost contains nutrients and trace elements such as iron, manganese, zinc, and copper that plants need to stay healthy, and it locks them into the

A Closer Look

The National Outdoor Leadership School recommends designing menus to eliminate food waste altogether. As you move toward that goal, also examine other alternatives: Donate unused food to food banks and charities, or feed food scraps to farm animals—your own or a nearby farmer's. Before you do, however, contact your local health department to find out whether the law permits it, and in what circumstances.

A Closer Look

If you plant fruits, vegetables, and annual flowers, you also need to add fertilizer to your compost. These plants grow quickly and need concentrated nutrients. Fertilizers emphasize three of these nutrients: nitrogen, potassium, and phosphorous, or N-P-K. Nitrogen promotes leaf growth; potassium and phosphorous promote stem and root growth. Ask your nursery person or county cooperative extension agent about the best fertilizer ratios and frequencies for your particular plants.

soil for gradual release over time. It also contains beneficial bacteria that enable plants to resist disease and viruses.

Equally important for keeping most plants healthy is good soil texture. The bulkiness of compost improves soil structure and texture and helps soil retain moisture. Think of compost as the complete vegetation health food meal!

THE COMPOSTING PROCESS

In the simplest terms, everyone is a composter. Each day, we eat food and drink water. Our bodies digest these products, using bacteria, acids, and enzymes. We absorb the nutrients we need, and then send the rest out as waste.

You can watch part of this process happen in a worm bin. In this box, where food scraps mix with dampened shredded paper, dry leaves, and straw, the worms eat through and leave nutrient-rich "soil" or "castings" behind.

The "hot" pile, or windrow method, allows you to watch the actual digestion process. The raw materials are yard wastes, or food scraps mixed with yard wastes. As you build the pile and turn it periodically with pitchforks, the wastes "cook down" (an explanation follows). The material then changes from a pile of many colors to a uniform earth brown, and shrinks to less than half the original size.

Neither the trench pit nor the cone method is as educational, because they're not easily observable. The first involves digging a trench or hole, mixing the scraps with dirt at the bottom, and covering them. The cone method involves digging a hole, setting a cone in place, and dropping the waste in until the hole is full. But whatever the method, the end product is still compost that you can add to planting beds or use as mulch for trees and shrubs.

In all methods, microbes start the composting digestion process by consuming carbon and nitrogen in the organic matter. Carbon is their energy source; nitrogen is their raw material for making proteins. Two types of microbes perform this digestion process: aerobic and anaerobic. The aerobic bacteria work in situations where there is plenty of oxygen: aerated piles and windrows, turning bins, and tumblers. Anaerobic bacteria work without oxygen, on buried wastes or where piles of debris become compressed and squeeze out the air. The aerobic microbes work with a minimum of odor, because of the circulating air, while anaerobic ones produce ammonia and other foul scents. You cannot smell the anaerobic bacteria if they are buried in pits or trenches, but you certainly can if they are out in the open, such as in rotting piles of grass.

After the microbes break down the dead tissues, fungi, protozoans, and other bacteria join in consuming the waste. Finally, insects and earthworms finish the job.

As the microbe population in a hot pile increases and then dies out, the heat of their work rises up to 160°F and falls, thus "cooking" the contents. This rise and fall takes a few days to complete. To restart the process, turn the pile using shovels and/or pitchforks, mixing the outside

A Closer Look

There are many books available on composting, but Stu Campbell's Let It Rot! *is probably the most readable for newcomers. You can use it to supplement what you read here. Likewise, for worm bins, start with Mary Applehof's* Worms Eat My Garbage.

Potential Pitfall

Do not try to handle the entire camp's output with your first composting project. The BBI camps tried that in 1990. By the end of the season, they had quite an achievement on their hands—they had handled more than 90 percent of their foodwaste output—but it was at quite a cost in staff friction. BBI hadn't predicted how much time and effort a project this size would take in personnel, programming, and coordination.

Programming Idea

❑ *Put on a rubber glove and stick a meat, candy, or darkroom thermometer into a hot pile to measure the heat.*

❑ *Mark the progress of the composting process as the temperature rises and falls.*

layer into the middle and middle layer outside. (Or, you can wait and turn the pile at the end of each week.) For best results, build a pile that occupies at least one cubic yard—3 feet high by 3 feet at the base. This size insulates itself and holds that heat.

Everything organic has a ratio of carbon to nitrogen (C:N) in its tissues. In composting language, items high in carbon are known as brown materials or bedding; those high in nitrogen are green. Brown-to-green ratios range from 500:1 for sawdust to 15:1 for table scraps. A 30:1 ratio is ideal for microbes to make quick work of breaking down the pile into compost.

In piles and windrows, the basic recipe for a 30:1 C:N ratio is two parts green grass clippings to one part fallen (dead, dry) leaves. Food scraps are also nitrogen-rich, but you may need to do some testing because they contain both brown (peanut shells, onion skins, tea bags, etc.) and green (fruits, vegetables, breads, pastas, etc.) materials. Start with one part food scraps to two parts bedding, or one part food to one part sawdust (fir or pine, not aromatics such as cedar, redwood, citrus, or eucalyptus, which decompose slowly), and observe how the pile cooks. Then, use the Troubleshooting Guide in this chapter to add or subtract bedding and moisture for the perfect mix.

If you choose a "hot" pile for your camp's composting effort, you can add weeds and vines, such as morning glory and ivy, as long as you chop them up finely with a lawn mower (even better, leave them out for a week to turn brown, then add them to the pile as bedding). The roots of these plants contain chlorophyll, which enables them while they are still green to generate new shoots from almost any point above or below ground. So, if you put 2–inch or longer segments of these roots into your compost pile, you run the risk of the plant growing through it.

Generally, the heat in a hot pile kills weed seeds, and bakes out chlorophyll in root bits. However, if you choose a cool pile (one you don't turn), keep the roots and weeds out.

A COMPOSTING EXAMPLE

The following steps demonstrate BBI's 1990 approach. You may wish to adapt for your camp's needs some or all of the procedures here:

1. Decide the scope of your composting efforts before camp begins, plan the steps to take, and equip the appropriate areas.
2. During orientation week, brief and rehearse all parties in "dry runs."
3. Collect food scraps from the kitchen prep area and dining hall, and provide buckets at each table for vegetable scraps (meat and dairy scraps, large fruit pits, and table papers go in the garbage). Perform the routines planned for table clearing and for food scrap sorting when the buckets are returned to the kitchen.
4. Locate three 30- to 50-gallon trash cans on wheels in each kitchen. (BBI filled one or two every day with 150 to 180 pounds of food waste each.) Transport filled cans daily by pickup truck to the composting site, a 1,000 square-foot space some distance away from the main camp buildings.

A Closer Look

Common brown, or bedding materials include coarse sawdust; peat moss; brown leaves, newspaper, or corrugated cardboard shredded in 1- to 2-inch-wide strips.

A Closer Look

Before implementing a composting program, be sure to coordinate all personnel who will be involved: the kitchen staff, the maintenance staff, the programming staff.

5. Compost these 3,000 to 4,000 pounds of scraps each week, selecting one or both of the following options:

❑ Windrow (above ground) method: Using either a front loader or camp shovels and pitchforks, mix each new load of waste with bedding material at a one-part-food to two-parts-bedding ratio on arrival. At the end of each week or two, turn the whole pile.

❑ Trench method: Using either a tractor backhoe or plenty of people with shovels and pitchforks, dig 1-foot-deep trenches, mix the scraps with 4 inches of dirt, and then refill the trench with 8 inches of soil.

Before BBI leaders could succeed, they had to spend extra time training staff and campers in the new procedures, equip the dining hall and kitchen for scrap collections, arrange for the camp's pickup truck to transport kitchen scraps to the windrow site, and pull labor from other jobs and programs to turn the pile.

Large-scale projects can be valuable additions to your camp programs, and they can be quite cost effective. But they take long-term planning, equipment, and good management, and should be attempted only after you are confident in your small- and moderate-scale successes. Use Worksheet 9–1: Composting Checklist at the end of this chapter to guarantee your success.

COMPOSTING OPTIONS

A Closer Look

❑ *Do compost vegetable materials, cereals, grains, landscape wastes, and shredded woody wastes and papers.*

❑ *Do not compost meat or fish parts (unless you grind them up finely), dairy products, or oils. Also, keep out diseased plants, invasive weeds (ivy, quack grass, morning glory, buttercup, etc.), weed seeds, and other high-nitrogen materials— unless, of course, you have a hot pile.*

Your composting options include:

❑ Pits or trenches, for food composting;

❑ Cones, which are open-ended containers placed over pits;

❑ Worm bins, which are basically an ant farm with worms that consume food wastes;

❑ Hot piles and windrows (extended piles), used for yard wastes or a combination of yard and food wastes;

❑ Bins, either the holding or turning varieties, for landscape wastes;

❑ Tumblers, which are cylinders on rollers for quick turning and composting of yard and/or food wastes.

For budget purposes, figure on spending $100 to $1,000 for basic equipment, depending on which method you choose. Your costs will be low if you choose worm bins, or a small yard-waste pile. Costs increase as you expand your scale.

As costs rise, you are obliged to calculate whether they are offset by (1) the costs you avoid for trash hauling, and buying fertilizers and other soil amendments; (2) the value you achieve from greater planting productivity; (3) the experience value for staff and campers; or (4) a combination of these and other factors.

PITS AND TRENCHES

Pits and trenches are neat and odor-free methods for food composting (see Figures 9–1 and 9–2). It's the same process many people used when

A Quick Summary

Pits or trenches:

❏ *Are odor-free.*

❏ *Decompose anaerobically within six months.*

❏ *Are for food and/or yard waste.*

❏ *Accept small amounts of waste.*

❏ *Are not a good visual demonstration because the process happens underground.*

they camped in the wild: Dig holes in the ground for garbage (and for latrines), then cover them with dirt to keep animals and pests away. The National Outdoor Leadership School now frowns on this method in camping as disruptive to wilderness ecosystems, and recommends that campers pack out everything they pack in.

At camp, however, depending on how much the land has already been "civilized" with planting beds and landscaping, you might use pits or trenches even on a large scale. The covered wastes decompose anaerobically within six months. Food buried this season provides soil amendment and nutrients for your vegetation next season. Do your composting in areas where you plan to raise plants, shrubs, or trees.

Figure 9-1. Pit composting method

TECHNIQUE Pits and trenches can be dug near the mess hall or farther afield in a garden, tree grove, or other plant-growing area. When the composting process is finished, you can plant in the soil over the hole or trench.

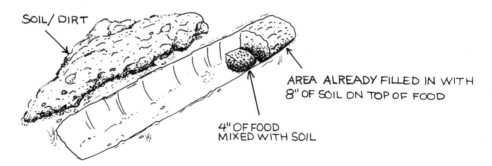

Figure 9-2. Trench composting method

The following steps must be done each time food scraps are brought out, to keep scavenging animals and insects at bay:

1. Dig a hole or trench at least 1 foot deep.
2. Fill the hole no more than 4 inches deep with food scraps.
3. Mix the scraps with dirt at the bottom of the hole or trench.
4. Cover the mix with 8 inches of dirt.

You'll need the following equipment, personnel, and time allotments:

❑ Ten square feet of space (which will accommodate a 2-foot x 5-foot trench or a 3-foot x 3-foot hole) near the dining hall or in a planting area or tree grove.

❑ Collection container(s) for the food scraps.

❑ Shovels to dig the hole or trench, mix the scraps with dirt, then cover the mix with more dirt.

❑ Transportation for the food scrap containers from the kitchen to the composting site.

❑ Rubber heavy-duty gloves, for kitchen people handling the food scraps, and workers at compost site. Workers at the dig site can also use gardening gloves.

❑ Two to six people to do the collection, digging, and mixing/covering work.

❑ Fifteen to 20 minutes to perform the transport, digging, and covering process each time.

CONES

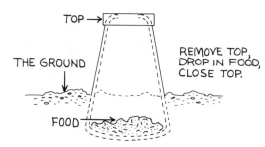

Figure 9-3. Cone composting method

Cones resemble upside-down, heavy-duty garbage cans with holes at both ends, or upside-down ice-cream cones, that you place over holes dug in the ground (see Figure 9-3). Several brands of cones are available from hardware, houseware and building supply emporiums, and mail order catalogs (see Appendix A for additional information).

When set in its hole, a cone stands 3 or 4 feet high. The narrower top of the cone has a cover, and the wider bottom, which fits into the pit, has either perforated sides or a mesh basket hanging below it. This basket is to keep moles and other underground rodents from getting in the compost. The model with the perforated sides is better because you don't have to handle the basket if you plan to move the cone.

Each cone accepts approximately one pound of material per day, or seven pounds per week. You should not have to move the cone unless you are composting in an impermeable, heavy clay soil. The anaerobic bacteria breaking down the material actually takes care of the bulk by helping the new soil to migrate beyond the hole where the cone is sitting. A heavy clay soil does not allow this absorption or migration.

Some cones come with a package of "accelerator" or "activator," which the manufacturer recommends to speed the composting process. Your green and brown ingredients contain all the bacteria necessary to commence the composting process. The speed of decomposition depends on the mix of carbon and nitrogen, and the type of process you perform. However, try the activator to see how well it works for your particular compost.

A Quick Summary

Cones:

❑ *Are fairly odor-free.*

❑ *Decompose anaerobically within six weeks.*

❑ *Are for food and/or yard waste.*

❑ *Accept only small amounts of waste at one time, about one pound per week.*

❑ *Are not a good visual demonstration because the process happens underneath the cone.*

TECHNIQUE Like the pit method, the cone method can be used near the dining hall or further afield in a garden or tree grove area. To ready the area for planting, the composting process takes at least six weeks to finish—after you remove the cone and cover the food scraps with dirt. Then, you can plant in the soil over the hole the following season. For best results:

1. Purchase two cones. Dig a pit for each, according to the instructions for the particular design (usually 18 inches to 3 feet deep and 24 inches to 42 inches wide).

2. Set the cones in their holes, pack dirt around the bases to seal them in place, and set the lids on top. Place a weight on each lid to discourage animals from getting in.

3. As you produce scraps from the kitchen, use them to fill one cone until you reach its capacity. (The capacity is the size of its base pit.)

4. When the base pit of the first cone is full, start filling the second cone. Leave the first cone dormant for about a week. When its scrap pile settles below the top of the basket or pit, remove it, cover the food pit with dirt, dig another pit, and reset the first cone. When the second cone is filled to capacity, start filling the first cone again, pull the second after a week, and reset it.

You'll need the following equipment, personnel, and time allotments:

❑ Nine square feet of space for each cone, placed near kitchen/dining hall.

❑ Cone(s).

❑ Shovel(s) for digging hole(s).

❑ Collection container(s) for food scraps.

❑ Rubber heavy-duty gloves for handling scraps.

❑ Twenty minutes and one or two people to dig each hole and set up each cone; then as cone bases fill with scraps every few weeks, to dig pits and set new cones.

❑ Ten minutes and one or two kitchen people every day to collect food scraps from kitchen and empty scraps into cone(s).

WORM BINS

Worm bins (see Figure 9-4) are an entertaining and educational way to handle several pounds of food scraps a week during the season. They create little mess and odor, and delight campers who enjoy getting their hands in their work.

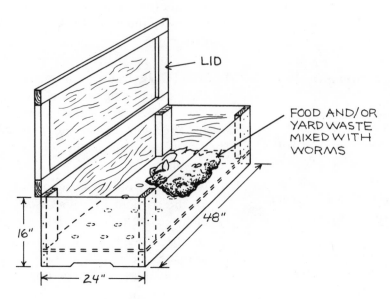

LID

FOOD AND/OR
YARD WASTE
MIXED WITH
WORMS

16"

48"

24"

Figure 9-4. Worm bin

A Quick Summary

Worm Bins:

❏ *Are fairly odor-free if you keep up the bedding supply.*

❏ *Are for food and/or yard waste.*

❏ *Entertain and provide a good demonstration because the process is visible.*

❏ *Accept at least 8 pounds of waste per week.*

❏ *Require bedding material.*

❏ *Produce good soil additive within six to eight weeks.*

Red worms are the digesters here. As the "green" food scraps decompose with the bedding, the worms eat the organic materials. They are different from "night crawlers," which live on mineral soils. If you cannot find a local red worm supplier, check Appendix A.

You need 1 to 2 pounds of worms for the average-sized bin—2-feet deep, and 2 or 3 feet x 4 feet. Worms reproduce quickly; a few score can multiply to over 1,500 in six months. Once your system is established, there will be plenty of worms to expand to other bins, and to use as fishing bait, if that is part of your camp program.

The key to a successful worm bin is surface area, not depth. Worms live and breathe near the earth's surface, so no worm bin should be more than 2 feet deep. Bins should be sized to provide 1 square foot of surface area for each pound of food waste added per week. For example, a 2 foot x 4 foot box handles 8 pounds of kitchen scraps a week, roughly what two or three adults produce.

The bin should be a sturdy wooden box with a tight-fitting lid. The tight lid keeps pets and rodents out, and protects the worms. To keep flies out, cover the bedding with a black plastic trash bag.

Fill the box to the top with bedding. If you try to compost food wastes without bedding, you'll get a slimy, smelly mess. Worms need a damp environment to survive, so bedding must be soaked and lightly wrung out before you place it in the bin. Any extra water drips out the holes in the bottom. Common bedding materials include coarse sawdust, hay, peat moss, and brown leaves mixed with newspaper or corrugated cardboard shredded in 1- to 2-inch wide strips.

TECHNIQUE For best results, follow these steps:

1. Build box(es).

2. Buy red worms (not night crawlers), 1 pound per 4 to 8 square feet of surface area.

3. Collect enough bedding material to fill the box to the top when the bedding is damp.

4. Fill a large tub with water.

5. Dampen the bedding, drain or squeeze out excess water, and place it loosely in the bin until the bin is full.

6. Add the worms.

7. Wait two days, and then add food scraps (vegetable matter, bread, grains, pastas, legumes, coffee filters, and tea bags—*not* bones, meat, fish, oils, or dairy products) at the rate of approximately 1 pound per square foot of surface area per day.

8. To add scraps, dig near the point where you buried the worms, add the pound of scraps, then cover it with several inches of bedding to prevent flies and odors from becoming a problem.

9. Rotate burial places in the bin to encourage migration of worms throughout the compost and create soil throughout the bin.

10. After six to eight weeks, harvest the compost castings, or new soil. Push the nearly finished soil to one side of the bin, then put fresh bedding and scraps in the empty side. For the next six weeks, bury food wastes in the newly bedded side only. The worms will migrate there as they finish the original side, leaving behind dark, crumbly, finished soil.

To harvest worms from your bin for fishing or other worm composting bins, open the bin and remove a shovelful of compost. Place the compost on a large piece of plastic (a lawn trash bag will do) in the sun or under a bright, warm light. The worms will migrate away from the heat. Let the pile sit in the heat for 10 minutes, then pull away the outer inch or two of compost until you see worms. To concentrate the worms into an even smaller pile, let the pile sit for another 10 minutes, then remove another layer of compost. Repeat the procedure until all the worms are at the bottom of the pile for easy harvesting.

You'll need the following space, equipment, personnel, and time allotments:

❏ Eight square feet of space for each bin, indoors or outdoors in a shady, relatively cool place.

❏ Worm boxes: wood, nails, hammer, hinges, screws, screw driver, drill, drill bits, etc. from design/materials list (see Appendix C).

❏ Worms.

❏ Water source near worm bin area for wetting materials.

❏ Bedding material.

❏ No-meat, no-fat food scraps.

❏ Rubber gloves (optional) for handling worms and wet bedding materials.

A Quick Summary

Hot piles or windrows:

❑ *Are primarily for yard waste, or a food and yard waste mixture.*

❑ *Handle from a few pounds to several tons of waste per week.*

❑ *Require more physical labor.*

❑ *Produce good soil additive within as little as two weeks.*

❑ *Are fairly odor-free if fresh material is mixed daily and piles are turned regularly.*

❑ *Provide a good visual demonstration of the composting process.*

HOT PILES AND WINDROWS

Hot piles and windrows (extended hot piles) are used primarily for yard and landscape wastes, or a mix of food and landscape wastes. They can be left free-standing, or contained in enclosures made of wood, wood and wire, plastic or wire mesh, or concrete blocks (see Figure 9-5).

They handle any food waste quantity from a pound to several tons a week. As quantities increase, however, you need more space and labor or mechanical equipment to handle the mixing and turning processes.

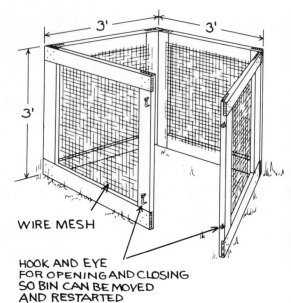

WIRE MESH

HOOK AND EYE
FOR OPENING AND CLOSING
SO BIN CAN BE MOVED
AND RESTARTED

Figure 9-5. Holding bin for hot piles and windrows

Hot piles and windrow composting methods enable you to create usable compost in as little as two weeks, by using fast-acting aerobic bacteria to cook nitrogen-rich green materials with carbon-rich brown materials. The changes you'll observe can be compared to a banana skin. As the banana ages, the skin turns from raw green to mellow yellow to blackish brown. This color change from light to dark brown is what you seek to achieve in a hot compost pile as you "cook" your food scraps.

You keep the "fire" going by regularly turning the pile in on itself and adding green material as needed. Turning aerates the pile, keeping aerobic bacteria at work. It also prevents the pile from compressing, squeezing out air, and letting anaerobic bacteria develop too early in the process, which yields ammonia and other bad odors.

Because food is particularly sensitive, you must handle it properly or it rots, smells terrible, and draws insects, rodents, and scavenging birds. For best results, follow these directions:

1. To maintain good sanitation, keep kitchen food-collection bins covered to keep odors in and insects out. Full bins must be delivered to the compost site at least every two days, but daily trips are better.

2. If you plan to compost every organic scrap that comes through your kitchen(s), collect them in heavy-duty, foodservice-model garbage cans on wheels or dollies. Otherwise, the filled bins will be too heavy to handle. The cans should also be a different shape or color from regular garbage cans to avoid confusion. Both Toter® and Rubbermaid® make square bins in sizes ranging from 25 to 50 gallons.

3. Ask the pickup crew to transport the bins to your composting area, empty them on the pile, wash out the bins, and return them to the

kitchen(s). Your compost site must be placed near a water source for this purpose and to enable you to moisten the pile regularly.

4. Each new load of food scraps taken to the hot pile must be mixed on the spot with an equal or double amount of brown material (e.g., hay, leaves, sawdust, damp shredded paper) at the moment the green is added to the pile. Allow no food scraps to show in the finished mixed pile.

5. Mixers must make certain the mixed ingredients are as consistently damp as a wrung-out sponge.

6. Put no meat or dairy scraps or large fruit pits in the pile.

7. The pile or windrow must be turned regularly (when heat dissipates) to keep it "hot" and cooking. This will be about every week to 10 days.

Treat hot piles as a batch process: Each time you build one to a height of 3 or 4 feet, start another one. One cubic yard is the optimum size that enables the pile to insulate itself for cooking. To create a windrow, simply start the next pile at the edge of the first, or previous one, in effect building a long line of piles.

In the static pile, which is used for landscape trimmings, heap up the items and let them decompose on their own. The mounds can be left free-standing, or contained in mesh or other enclosures (see Appendix C for designs). The soonest you'll get usable compost with this method is about six months. If it produces an odor, refer to the Troubleshooting Guide in this chapter for remedies.

The hot pile process can take two to four weeks to complete, which means its period may include two or three camp sessions. Campers who start the first batch may not be there to see it finish. For program continuity, start a hot pile each week of each session. This gives participants the opportunity to be involved in each part of the composting process. Make sure campers have the chance to do all of the following:

❑ Collect and mix the materials, and create the pile.
❑ Turn the pile and add new green at least once.
❑ Learn how to use appropriate tools.
❑ Learn about composting and other natural processes (i.e., the Earth's carbon and water cycles).
❑ Realize that even though they may not see the conclusion of their work, they've made an important contribution that will benefit those who come after them.

If your program operates during the summer only, simply leave all the piles that have been started. They'll become static over the winter, and decompose by themselves into usable compost over those several months. Returning participants can see the results of the previous season's work, distribute the compost as mulch for plants and amendment for gardening soils, and start anew for the coming season.

TECHNIQUE To implement hot pile composting, follow these guidelines:

1. Collect nitrogen-rich green and carbon-rich brown materials.

2. If you are doing yard wastes only, stockpile them until you collect enough to make your first pile. Do not use aromatic leaves or woods such as eucalyptus, citrus, cedar, or redwood as brown material. The pungent oils in these materials dramatically slow the decomposition process.

3. If you are combining food with yard wastes, you must mix the food waste (green) with brown materials immediately. Yard wastes can be stockpiled, but food wastes cannot without creating unsanitary conditions: they rot, smell, and attract rodents, scavenging birds, or insects.

4. Mix green and brown materials at a ratio of one part green to two parts brown. Refer to the Troubleshooting Guide in this chapter to correct your mix if problems occur (for example, if you can't keep up the heat—or if the pile produces odors. Food wastes require closer observation than yard waste, so you may have to correct the ratio of the mix.)

5. Dampen the materials as you mix them until they are as damp as a wrung-out sponge. Try not to over-water or under-water them.

6. Over the next few days, check the temperature of the pile with your hand in a rubber glove, or with a thermometer. Over a period of three to six days, you should see heat rise and fall as the bacterial action progresses.

7. When the heat dissipates (at four to seven days), turn the pile to rekindle the process, and add more green material if you don't feel heat. Over two to four weeks, (a) the colors in the pile change to a uniform dark brown, (b) the pile cooks down to half its original size, (c) the scent of the pile changes from a mix of odors to a single, earthy smell, and (d) the pile heats less each time you turn it.

8. If you are proceeding with more than a demonstration pile, each time you build one pile up 3 to 4 feet, start another adjacent to it. This way, you create a long row of these piles. Turn each according to its heat cycle.

You need the following equipment, personnel, and time allotments:

❏ From 100 to 400 square feet of space, depending on the scope of piles or windrows, at least 50 yards from camp activity areas.

❏ Shovel(s) for digging and transferring materials.*

❏ Pitchfork(s) for mixing and turning materials.*

❏ Wheelbarrow(s) for transporting materials.*

❏ Water source near pile area for wetting materials.

❏ Method for collecting and delivering yard waste:
   30-gallon, wheeled trash cans,
   5-, 7- or 10-gallon bins,
   Wheelbarrow(s) for transport, or
   Camp pickup truck

❏ Heavy-duty rubber gloves for handling scraps.

*A front loader can be used for all of these functions.

❑ Ten to 30 minutes periodically to collect materials, transfer them to the pile, and mix them in.

❑ Ten to 60 minutes once a week to turn the pile(s) or windrow(s).

TURNING BINS

A Quick Summary

Turning bins:

❑ *Handle three smaller loads at different stages at one time.*

❑ *Produce good soil additive in three to four weeks.*

❑ *Are a fairly good demonstration of the composting process.*

❑ *Require labor for regular turning.*

❑ *Are for food and yard waste.*

Turning bins are a series of 1 cubic yard (3- x 3- x 3-foot) bins in a single frame that enable you to hot compost yard and landscape wastes one batch at a time. These bins can be made of wood, wood and wire, plastic or wire mesh, or concrete blocks (see Figure 9-6). You can build these bin frames as camp projects or buy them ready-made (the materials list is on the illustration in Appendix C; see Appendix A supplier list). Turning bins enable you to turn the wastes regularly, which aerates them to give the bacteria plenty of oxygen to do their work.

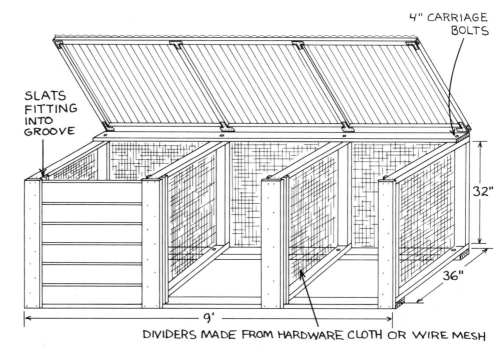

Figure 9-6. Turning bin

TECHNIQUE For best results, follow these steps:

1. Build or purchase three bins.

2. Stockpile green and brown yard and landscape wastes until there is enough to fill one bin. Mix them together at a ratio of one part green to two parts brown material. Dampen them with water until they are as wet as a wrung-out sponge, then load the wastes in the first bin.

3. Monitor by hand or with a thermometer in bin one as the heat rises and falls. (This should take about a week.) After the heat decreases, turn the mixture into the next bin (number two) and check its moisture content. Add water, if necessary, and green material if you don't feel heat.

4. Reload material from your stockpile into the first bin. Dampen the materials if they are not moist.

5. After the pile in bin two heats and starts to cool again (another week), turn it into bin three, turn the materials from bin one into bin two, and refill bin one. Add water to any bin that needs it.

6. After another 7 to 10 days, the compost in bin three should be ready for garden use. Turn it out and reload the other bins.

You need the following equipment, personnel, and time allotments:

❑ From 150 to 200 square feet of space, which can be close to camp activity areas.

❑ Turning bin *frames*: wood and/or chicken wire or hardware cloth, nails, staples, hammer, hinges, screws, screwdriver, drill, and drill bits, from design materials list in Appendix C.

❑ Water source near frame area to wet materials.

❑ Hose with spray nozzle, or a watering can.

❑ Shovel(s) and pitchfork(s) for mixing and turning materials.

❑ Heavy-duty garden or rubber gloves, for handling scraps.

❑ Method for collecting and delivering yard waste:
Wheelbarrow(s) for transport,
Camp pickup truck.

❑ Ten to 30 minutes periodically to collect materials, transfer, and mix them into stockpile.

❑ Ten to 30 minutes once each week or two to turn materials through bins.

A *Quick Summary*

Tumbler bins:

❑ *Handle 150 pounds of material per batch.*

❑ *Produce usable compost in as little as two weeks.*

❑ *Are for food and/or yard waste.*

❑ *Provide poor visual demonstration.*

Program Idea

You can construct a tumbler as a camp arts and crafts or shop project using a 55-gallon drum on a frame with rollers. Some metal-cutting, sawing, drilling, and welding may be required. The 55-gallon size handles approximately 150 pounds of compostable materials per batch.

TUMBLER BINS

Tumbler bins are designed for fast mixing and fast decomposing of batches of green and brown materials, just like the bin methods (see Figure 9-7). Tumblers are available in several sizes and prices, and can handle kitchen and yard wastes separately, or combined.

Tumblers are as fast as, or faster than, hot piles, turning out finished product in as little as two weeks. However, each tumbler has a finite capacity, and after it is loaded, each batch must be processed to completion, just as with hot piles and turning bins.

Also, until one batch finishes composting, additional waste material must be stockpiled, just as with the turning bins. But remember: you cannot stockpile food scraps as you can yard wastes, so you may use food scraps only on the day you begin a new tumbler—throw the food away on the other days or use another composting method to dispose of it.

TECHNIQUE Follow these steps for best results:

1. Build or purchase at least one tumbler.

2. Place tumbler at least 20 yards from camp activity areas.

3. Stockpile brown and green materials (no food) until you have enough to fill one tumbler. Collect and add food only when you are ready to load the tumbler. If you decide to compost food only, mix the first batch one-to-two with brown material to start, then add more brown, if needed, until you find your best mix.

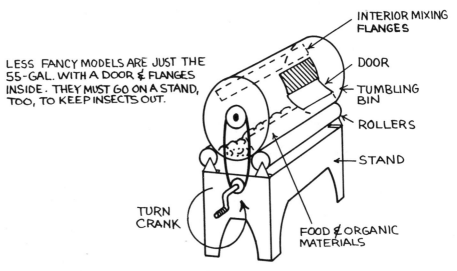

LESS FANCY MODELS ARE JUST THE 55-GAL. WITH A DOOR & FLANGES INSIDE. THEY MUST GO ON A STAND, TOO, TO KEEP INSECTS OUT.

INTERIOR MIXING FLANGES

DOOR

TUMBLING BIN

ROLLERS

STAND

TURN CRANK

FOOD & ORGANIC MATERIALS

Figure 9-7. Tumbler bin

A Closer Look

Using a lawn mower to chop wastes dulls the mower blade. There are fancier machines on the market, and suppliers are listed in Appendix A. Also, if you insist on adding meat or fish products to your compost, you must grind them up, then mix them thoroughly with brown material such as sawdust before adding them to any batch.

4. Load the standard ratio of one part green to two parts brown into the tumbler, filling it to capacity. If necessary, adjust the mix according to the Troubleshooting Guide in this chapter. Dampen materials in each batch until they feel like a wrung-out sponge.

5. Turn the tumbler a number of times. Repeat this action daily for 10 days to 2 weeks after capacity is reached, checking the heat each time. Add more green material at about 4 and 8 days as the heat from the cooking load decreases during the composting period, then let heat dissipate until the end of the two weeks.

6. Empty the tumbler's contents and stockpile this mulch to use on planting beds or groves.

7. Refill tumbler with green and brown raw materials.

You need the following space, equipment, personnel, and time allotments:

❑ Fifty square feet of space for tumbler, stockpiles of raw materials, and finished compost.

❑ Water source near tumbler.

❑ Fifty-five-gallon drum, structural components, welding equipment, and woodworking equipment, if you plan to build, or ready-to-use manufactured tumbler system.

❑ Shovels for digging materials, and loading and emptying tumbler.

❑ Pitchforks for mixing green and brown materials.

❑ Wheelbarrow for transporting materials.

❏   Rubber or garden gloves for handling materials.

A shredder or grinder may come in handy to chop woody wastes, such as tree branches and corn stalks, and tough food wastes, such as corn cobs and melon rinds. Usually, a rotary lawn mower will suffice for this purpose. For camp liability purposes, this task should be completed by one of the staff, not by campers.

TROUBLESHOOTING GUIDE

This general guide to composting will help you troubleshoot the most common compost challenges. Thanks go to the Seattle (Washington) Tilth and Seattle Solid Waste Utility for supplying this list.

SYMPTOM	PROBLEMS	SOLUTION
Bad odor	Not enough air; pile too wet; not enough bedding	Turn compost, add coarse dry materials such as straw, corn stalk, newspaper
Ammonia	Too much nitrogen (green material)	Add brown material
Rotten egg	Anaerobic; too much water	Turn or add drier materials to encourage aerobic bacteria
Center of pile is dry	Not enough water; too much woody, coarse material	Turn and moisten materials; add fresh green wastes and shredded coarse wastes
Compost is only damp and warm in the middle, nowhere else	Pile too small	Collect more material and mix into the existing compost
Heap is damp and sweet-smelling but still doesn't heat	Lack of nitrogen	Mix in a nitrogen source such as fresh grass clippings, fresh manure, bloodmeal, or ammonium sulfate

FINAL THOUGHTS

Composting is an excellent way both to prevent adding solid wastes to our landfills and to cut down on fertilizers and other poisonous chemicals we use in landscaping. Although composting requires more up-front preparation than other environmental programs, the end results are worth the efforts.

Overall, be patient and persevere in your environmental efforts. If you are tempted to quit, ask yourself, "What kind of example would quitting on the environment set for my camp?" Then, keep up the good work!

WORKSHEET 9-1
COMPOSTING CHECKLIST

Check each step as you complete it.

_____ Before the season begins, research available methods and decide how to proceed. Call an advisor such as a city or county master composter, a knowledgeable organic farmer, or your county cooperative extension agent.

_____ Win support from the camp director, board, kitchen manager, and grounds crew or permanent staff.

_____ Determine the scale and the budget for the composting program.

_____ Determine how to schedule the activities into the programs.

_____ Equip and make space in appropriate area(s) for the chosen composting method.

_____ Add to kitchen manager's job description: Separate compostables from recyclables and garbage; coordinate, with the grounds crew or counselor(s), regular pickups from the kitchen for removal to the compost pile, windrow, trench, worm bin, or farm feed lot.

_____ Train the kitchen manager and prep staff in new routine(s) for chosen compost method.

_____ If doing a large scale program, add to the grounds crew's job description: Coordinate, with the kitchen manager, pickups of compostables for removal to the composting site or farm feed lot.

_____ Check with your health department to find out if local codes permit giving away food scraps to local farms. If so, (1) what kinds of scraps, (2) in what form, and (3) in what circumstances.

_____ At orientation, brief staff and counselors, demonstrate method, rehearse, and invite input in order to create ownership and enthusiasm to make the program work.

_____ At the camp's first meal, introduce campers to the new system, and let counselors manage the details at each table and sleeping unit.

4
APPENDICES

APPENDIX A: RESOURCES

CATALOG RESOURCES

American Camping Association, Inc.
5000 State Road 67 North
Martinsville, IN 46151-7902
(317) 342-8456

Camp and Program Leader Catalog of over 500 outdoor and environmental education resource books.

Conari Press
1144 65th Street, Suite B
Emeryville, CA 94608
(800) 685-9595

Focused on saving the Earth, Earth Cards (postcards) you can sign and send.

Eco-Choice
P.O. Box 281
Montvale, NJ 07645-0281
(800) 535-6304

Conservation and eco-friendly equipment and products.

Eco Source
P.O. Box 1656
Sebastopol, CA 95473
(800) 274-7040

Household and personal eco-friendly products.

Flowerfield Enterprises
10332 Shaver Road
Kalamazoo, MI 49002
(616) 327-0108

Equipment and books for vermicomposting. Red worm source.

The Green Spirit
P.O. Box 816
New Albany, IN 47151-0816
(800) 942-4383

Environmentally friendly composting, cleaning, and personal hygiene products.

Island Press
P.O. Box 7
Covelo, CA 95428
(800) 828-1302

Books on environmental issues.

National Coalition Against the Misuse of Pesticides
701 E Street S.E., Suite 200
Washington, DC 20003
(202) 543-5450

Books and position statements on toxic issues.

Nature Watch
P.O. Box 1668
Reseda, CA 91337
(818) 340-0386

Activities, and arts and crafts materials from nature.

Real Goods
966 Mazzoni Street
Ukiah, CA 95482-3471
(800) 762-7325

Alternative energy products, and conservation and recycled materials products.

Seventh Generation
Colchester, VT 05446-1672
(800) 456-1177

Conservation and recycled materials products. Please send $2 for catalog.

Tom Snyder Productions
80 Coolidge Hill Road
Watertown, MA 02172
(617) 876-4433

Educational software for teaching environment and race issues, and standard subjects.

PRINTED RESOURCES

Hazardous and Toxic Materials

Environmental Hazards Management Institute, 1992. *Household Hazardous Waste Wheel*. Durham, NH: Environmental Hazards Management Institute.

Cardstock information wheel with answers about toxicity levels, and handling, storage, and disposal of toxics. Available from American Camping Association.

Ibid. *Recycle Information Wheel*. Durham, NH: Environmental Hazards Management Institute.

Cardstock information wheel with answers to questions about recycling. Available from American Camping Association.

Greenpeace. *Stepping Lightly on the Earth: Everyone's Guide to Toxics in the Home*. Washington, DC: Greenpeace, Inc.

Poster with resources and recipes for non-toxic household products.

National Coalition Against the Misuse of Pesticides, 1991. *Safety at Home: A Guide to Risks of Lawn and Garden Pesticides and Safer Ways to Manage Pests*. Washington, DC: National Coalition Against the Misuse of Pesticides.

Includes information on how to evaluate a program that advertises itself as organic lawn care.

U.S. Department of Health and Human Services, 1986. *Registry of Toxic Effects of Chemical Substances*. Washington, DC: U.S. Department of Health and Human Services.

Wylie, Harriet, 1980. *420 Ways to Clean Everything*. New York, NY: Harmony Books/Crown Publishers.

Alternatives to toxic and hazardous cleaning products.

Solid Waste and Composting

Appelhof, Mary, 1982. *Worms Eat My Garbage*. Kalamazoo, MI: Flower Press.

Directions and plans for vermicomposting.

BioCycle. Emmaus, PA: The JG Press, Inc.
Monthly magazine of solid waste management, concentrating on composting.

Campbell, Stu, 1989. *Let It Rot*. Pownal, VT: Storey Communications.
Composting ideas.

Duffield, Mary Rose, and Jones, Warren D., 1992. *Plants for Dry Climates: How to Select, Grow and Enjoy*. Los Angeles, CA: Price, Stern, Sloan.
Basic xeriscaping.

In Business. Emmaus, PA: The JG Press, Inc.
Bi-monthly magazine on environmentally related businesses and how to conduct business environmentally.

Organic Gardening. Emmaus, PA: Rodale Press.
Monthly journal of organic gardening, composting, and natural yard care.

National Soft Drink Association, 1991. *A National Directory of Solid Waste Curricula and Educational Resources*. Washington, DC: National Soft Drink Association.
Sixteen-page state-by-state listing of environmental curricula.

Proctor & Gamble Educational Services, 1992. *Planet Patrol*. Cincinnati, OH: Proctor & Gamble Educational Services.
An environmental unit on solid waste solutions for grades four to six.

Ibid. *Decision Earth*. Cincinnati, OH: Proctor and Gamble Educational Services.
An environmental unit on solid waste solutions for grades six to 12. Also includes life-cycle analysis of a consumer product.

Energy

American Camping Association, Inc., 1984. *Vehicle Log*. Martinsville, IN: American Camping Association, Inc.
Record of maintenance, repairs, gas mileage, and trip miles, for camp vehicles.

Consumer Reports. Yonkers, NY: Consumers Union of the U.S., Inc.
Monthly magazine of product tests and annual books.

Daniels, Farrington, 1964. *Direct Use of the Sun's Energy*. New Haven, CT: Yale University Press.
Technical handbook on solar energy.

Gas Appliance Manufacturers Association. *Consumer's Directory of Certified Efficiency Ratings for Residential Heating and Water Heating Equipment*. Courtland, NY: GAMA with ETL Testing Laboratories.
Bi-annual book available by subscription or in single copies.

Sardinsky, Robert, 1992. *The Efficient House Sourebook*. Snowmass, CO: Rocky Mountain Institute.
Directory of energy and water conservation resources. Includes designs and materials lists.

Stobaugh, Robert, and Yergin, Daniel, 1979. *Energy Future*. New York, NY: Ballantine.
Discussion of world energy politics.

Wilson, Alex, 1992. *Consumer Guide to Home Energy Savings*. Washington, DC: American Council for Energy-Efficient Economy.
Information on energy efficient appliances and heating systems.

Recycling

Bottle-Can Recycling Update. Portland, OR: Resource Recycling, Inc.
Trade periodical on recycling. Monthly newsletter.

Resource Recycling, Inc. *Directory of Plastics, Processors, and Buyers*. Portland, OR: Resource Recycling, Inc.
Annual guide to U.S. and Canadian plastics recycling.

The Plastics Recycling Update. Portland, OR: Resource Recycling, Inc.
Monthly newsletter.

Resource Recycling. Portland, OR: Resource Recycling, Inc.
A monthly magazine of the recycling industry.

Other Environmental Sources

American Camping Association, Inc., 1990. *Standards for Day and Resident Camps: The Accreditation Programs of the American Camping Association*. Martinsville, IN: American Camping Association, Inc.
Industry standards and their interpretations for camps in the areas of program, staff, food service, health care, site management, and administration.

Asimov, Isaac, 1977. *Animals of the Bible*. New York, NY: Doubleday.
Discussion of the animal kingdom as presented in the Bible.

Boy Scouts of America, 1992. *Boy Scout Handbook*. Irving, TX: Boy Scouts of America.

B.S.A. publishes books, study guides, and curricula on outdoor education for young men and women.

Buchman, Ellen, 1973. *Recipes for a Small Planet*. New York, NY: Ballantine Books.
Vegetarian recipes.

Camping Magazine. Martinsville, IN: American Camping Association, Inc.
Bi-monthly magazine for camp professionals and volunteers.

Carson, Rachel, 1956. *A Sense of Wonder*. New York, NY: Harper & Row.
Homage to the marvels of the natural world.

Ibid., 1967. *Silent Spring*. Boston, MA: Houghton-Mifflin.

Christensen, Karen, 1991. *Home Ecology: Simple and Practical Ways to Green Your Home*. Golden, CO: Fulcrum Publishers.
Advice on making the home environmentally friendly.

Co-op America Quarterly. Washington, DC: Co-op America.
Quarterly journal about environmental investments, actions, products and boycott news.

Cornell, Joseph, 1989. *Sharing the Joy of Nature*. Nevada City, CA: Dawn Publications.
His second activity book (see below).

Ibid., 1979. *Sharing Nature With Children*. Nevada City, CA: Dawn Publications.
Collection of classic activities for encouraging children to understand nature.

Earthworks Group, 1990. *50 Simple Things Kids Can Do To Save the Earth*. Berkeley, CA: Earthworks Group.
Everyday ways kids can make a difference.

Ibid., 1989. *50 Simple Things You Can Do To Save The Earth*. Berkeley, CA: Earthworks Group.
Everyday ways anyone can make a difference.

Ibid., 1990. *The Recycler's Handbook*. Berkeley, CA: Earthworks Group.
Reference work for novices and old hands alike.

Ford, Phyllis M., 1991. *Take A New Bearing: Skills and Sensitive Strategies for Sharing Spiders, Stars, Shelters, Safety and Solitude*. Martinsville, IN: American Camping Association, Inc.
The outdoor living skill handbook.

Girl Scouts of the U.S.A., 1984. *Outdoor Education in Girl Scouting*. New York, NY: Girl Scouts of the U.S.A.
G.S.U.S.A. publishes books, study guides, and curricula on outdoor education for young women.

Herman, Passineau, Schimpf, and Treuer, 1991. *Teaching Kids to Love the Earth*. Duluth, MN: Pfiefer-Hamilton Publishers.
Over 150 nature activities for parents and teachers.

Kennedy, Dreier, Bergeson, Nye, 1990. *Earth Matters: A Challenge for Environmental Action*. New York, NY: Girl Scouts of the U.S.A.
Discussion and activity ideas on environmental topics.

Klutztown Publishing, 1992. *Directory of Environmental Activities and Resources in the North American Religious Community*. Klutztown, PA: Klutztown Publishers.

Lanier-Graham, Susan D., 1991. *The Nature Directory: A Guide to Environmental Organizations*. New York, NY: Walker Publishers.
History of and contact information on 107 nature organizations.

Langone, John, 1981. *Thorny Issues: How Ethics and Morality Affect the Way We Live*. New York, NY: Little Brown and Company.
Essays on selected environmental issues.

Leopold, Aldo. 1976. *The Sand County Almanac*. New York, NY: Ballantine.

Lerner, Carol, 1982. *A Biblical Garden*. New York, NY: William Morrow.
Plants of the Bible.

Lewis, Barbara, 1991. *The Kid's Guide to Social Action*. Minneapolis, MN: Freespirit Press.
Creative ideas for solving social problems.

Linglebach, Jenepher, 1986. *Hands On Nature*. Woodstock, VT: Vermont Institute of Natural Science.
A classic for exploring the environment with children.

Petrash, Carol, 1992. *Earthways: Simple Environmental Activities for Young Children*. Mt. Rainier, MD: Gryphon House.
Simple ideas for bringing nature to young children.

Merchant, Carolyn, 1980. *The Death of Nature*. San Francisco, CA: Harper & Row.

Warning about the conflict between human development and the Earth's ability to adjust.

Miller, Lenore Hendler, 1988. *The Nature Specialist: A Complete Guide to Program and Activities*. Martinsville, IN: American Camping Association, Inc.
A complete how-to for the new or experienced naturalist.

Seventh Generation, 1990. *Seventh Generation's Field Guide to More Than 100 Environmental Groups*. Colchester, VT: Seventh Generation.
Directory.

Sheehan, Waiden, Lowry, 1991. *Earth Child: Games, Stories, Activities, Experiments and Ideas About Living Lightly on Planet Earth*. Tulsa, OK: Council Oaks Books.
A "new classic" for the environmental educator's bookshelf.

Solar Box Journal. Seattle, WA: Solar Box Cookers Northwest.
Journal of solar technologies.

Stewart's Green Line, annual. *The Environmental Directory*. Delta, BC: Stewart's Green Line.

Urban Wildlife Newsletter. Kirkland, WA: Urban Wildlife.
Quarterly newsletter available with membership.

VanMatre, Steve, 1972. *Acclimatization: A Sensory and Conceptual Approach to Ecological Involvement*. Martinsville, IN: American Camping Association, Inc.
Details of the original six-day earth education program from the master.

Ibid., 1979. *Sunship Earth: An Earth Education Program for Getting to Know Your Place in Space*. Martinsville, IN: American Camping Association, Inc.
Activities for helping children understand how their world functions.

YMCA Storer Camps, 1989. *Nature's Classroom: A Program for Camps and Schools*. Martinsville, IN: American Camping Association, Inc.
Over 40 outdoor programming activities.

NATIONAL ORGANIZATIONS WITH YOUTH AND CAMP PROGRAMS

American Camping Association, Inc.
5000 State Road 67 North
Martinsville, IN 46151-7902
(317) 342-8456

American Canoe Association
7432 Alban Station Boulevard, Suite B-226
Springfield, VA 22150-2311
(703) 451-0141

Hostelling International American Youth Hostels
P.O. Box 37613
Washington, DC 20013-7613
(202) 783-6161

Association for Experiential Education
2885 Aurora Avenue, Suite 8
Boulder, CO 80303
(303) 440-8844

Boy Scouts of America
1325 West Walnut Hill Lane
P.O. Box 152079
Irving, TX 75015-2079
(214) 580-2000

Camp Fire, Inc.
4601 Madison Avenue
Kansas City, MO 64112
(816) 756-1950

Catholic Youth Organization
910 Marion Street
Seattle, WA 98104
(206) 382-4562

Canadian Camping Association
1806 Avenue Road
Toronto, Ontario M5M 3Z1 Canada
(416) 791-4717

Christian Camping International U.S.A.
P.O. Box 646
Wheaton, IL 60189
(708) 462-0330

Coalition for Education Outdoors
P.O. Box 2000, Park Center
Cortland, NY 13045

Girl Scouts of the U.S.A.
420 Fifth Avenue
New York, NY 10022
(212) 852-8000

Jewish Community Center Association
15 East 26th Street
New York, NY 10010
(212) 532-4949

National 4-H Administrative Staff Group
ES - USDA, Room 3860 - S
Washington, DC 20250-0900
(202) 720-5516

National Outdoor Leadership School
Box AA
Lander, WY 82520
(307) 332-6973

Outward Bound U.S.A.
384 Field Point Road
Greenwich, CT 06830
(203) 661-0797

Note: Outward Bound will be moving in the spring of 1993.

Wilderness Education Association
20 Winona Avenue, Box 89
Saranac Lake, NY 12983
(518) 891-2915

YMCA of the U.S.A.
101 North Wacker Drive, 14th Floor
Chicago, IL 60606
(312) 977-0031

YWCA of the U.S.A.
726 Broadway, 5th Floor
New York, NY 10003
(212) 614-2700

NATIONAL ORGANIZATIONS WITH ENVIRONMENTAL INFORMATION

American Council for an Energy Efficient Economy
1001 Connecticut Avenue N.W., Suite 535
Washington, DC 20036
(202) 429-8873
(510) 549-9914 publications

American Forestry Association
Global Releaf Program
P.O. Box 2000
Washington, DC 20013
(202) 667-3300

Can Manufacturers Institute
1625 Massachusetts Avenue N.W.
Washington, DC 20036
(202) 232-4677
Provides nationwide recycling referral information.

Center for Marine Conservation
1725 DeSales Street N.W.
Washington, DC 20036
(202) 429-5609

Conservation and Renewable Energy Inquiry and Referral Service
P.O. Box 8900
Silver Spring, MD 20907
(800) 523-2929

Consumers Union of U.S., Inc.
101 Truman Avenue
Yonkers, NY 10703
(914) 378-2000
Monthly *Consumer Reports* of product tests and annual books.

Co-op America
2100 M Street N.W., Suite 403
Washington, DC 20037
(202) 872-5307
Tracks environmental investments, actions, products and boycott news.

Direct Marketing Association
Mail Preference Service
6 E. 43rd. Street
New York, NY 10017
Eliminates your name from bulk-mailing lists.

Environmental Hazards Management Institute
P.O. Box 932
Durham, NH 03824
(800) 446-5456

Glass Packaging Institute
1801 K Street N.W., Suite 1105 L
Washington, DC 20006
(202) 887-4850

Provides nationwide recycling referral information.

Greenpeace, Inc.
Greenpeace Information Services (for publications)
1436 U Street N.W.
Washington, DC 20009
(202) 462-8817

Illumination Engineering Society
345 East 47th Street
New York, NY 10017
(212) 705-7926

Institute for Urban Wildlife
10921 Trotting Ridge Way
Columbia, MD 21044
(410) 995-1119

Private non-profit organization dedicated to wildlife conservation, research management, and education about wildlife in urbanizing areas.

The Joint Appeal in Religion and Science
1047 Amsterdam Avenue
New York, NY 10025
(212) 316-7441

National Coalition Against the Misuse of Pesticides
701 E Street S.E., Suite 200
Washington, DC 20003
(202) 543-5450

National Recycling Coalition
1101 30th Street N.W., Suite 305
Washington, DC 20007
(202) 625-6406

Tracks recycling policies and developments.

National Renewable Energy Laboratory
1617 Cole Boulevard
Golden, CO 80401-3393
Quarterly magazine, contract research activities, and multi-media programs available.

National Soft Drink Association
1101 16th Street N.W.
Washington, DC 20036
(202) 463-6700
Provides nationwide recycling referral information.

National Wildlife Federation
1400 16th Street N.W.
Washington, DC 20036-2266
(703) 790-4233
Register to become a certified backyard wildlife sanctuary.

Occupational Safety and Health Administration (OSHA)
Room N-301 (Publications)
200 Constitution Avenue N.W.
Washington, DC 20210
To find one of the 10 regional OSHA offices, check the government listings in your phone book.

Resource Recycling
P.O. Box 10540
Portland, OR 97210
(503) 227-6135
Consultants and publishers of *Resource Recycling* the industry standard magazine. Annual issues are devoted to markets and equipment for recycling and composting.

Rocky Mountain Institute
1739 Snowmass Creek Road
Snowmass, CO 81654-9199
(303) 927-3128
Information and referrals on energy and water conservation systems and strategies.

Safe Energy Communication Council
1717 Massachusetts Avenue N.W., Suite LL-215
Washington, DC 20036
(202) 483-8491
Provides communications tools about energy efficiency, including opinions, efficiency reports, and camera-ready graphics. Publications list available.

Save the Rainforests
604 Jamie Street
Dodgeville, WI 53533
(608) 935-9435

Teachers guide to environmental action, including how schools can help save rainforests, and how students and teachers can attend courses conducted in the tropics.

Solid Waste Council
(800) 457-4474

Provides general composting information, and nationwide information referral.

Solid Waste Information Clearing House
(800) 677-9424

Provides general solid waste information, and acts as nationwide information referral.

Superfund/Resource Conservation and Recovery Act Information Hotline
(800) 424-9346

Call this number for information only—not for reporting spills.

World Watch Institute
1776 Massachusetts Avenue N.W.
Washington, DC 20036
(202) 452-1776

GOVERNMENT AND OTHER PUBLIC SERVICE RESOURCES

Look in the telephone book under government offices to find the service you need. Check city, county, state, and federal listings. The office that serves your particular need may be called something slightly different or be a department within a department, so look carefully. Here are suggestions of key words to look for:

Agriculture

Air and Water Pollution

Clean City Committee

   Recycle Hotline

Ecology/Environmental Quality

Environmental Management

   Solid Waste

   Hazardous Waste

   Water Quality

Environmental Protection Agency (EPA)
Fire Department (underground tanks)
Health and Hospital
   Asbestos
   Hazardous Material Management
   Health Department or District
   Sewage, Septic, and Wells
   Water Pollution
   Water Testing
Interior
   Fish and Wildlife
Natural Resources
   Fish and Wildlife
   Forestry
Public Works
   Drainage
   Garbage and Trash
   Heavy Trash
   Sewer
   Water and Land
OSHA

YELLOW PAGES RESOURCES

Look for these key words in the *Yellow Pages* directory to find related information:

Agriculture; chemicals
Air; conditioning, pollution control
Asbestos
Automobile; emission testing
Chemical
Containers; waste
Disposal; garbage, rubbish
Ecological Services
Energy
Environmental; conservation, services, testing
Fishing, bait
Garbage
Garden and Lawn
Glass; recycling
Hauling
Hazardous Waste

Infectious Waste
Lawn and Garden
Metal; recycling
Oils; waste
Paper; recycling
Plastics; recycling
Pollution
Radon Testing
Recycling
Rubbish
Scrap; metals, plastics
Soil; testing
Solar
Toxics
Trash
Waste
Water
Worms

FEDERAL LAWS AND RESOURCES ON HAZARDOUS AND TOXIC MATERIALS

U.S. Water Pollution Control Act; sections 102, 307, 311
Solid Waste Disposal Act; section 3001
Clean Air Act; section 112
40 Combined Federal Regulations (CFR); sections 261–263
Toxic Substances Control Act; section 7

U.S. Clean Air Act of 1990, PL 101–549.
U.S. Hazardous and Solid Waste Disposal Act of 1984, PL 98–616.
U.S. Toxic Substances Control Act of 1976, PL 92–500.
U.S. Water Pollution Control Act of 1976, PL 94–469.
Uniform Hazardous Waste Manifest, form 8700-22. *Code of Federal Regulations*, 261–268.

APPENDIX B: PUBLICIZING YOUR PROGRAM

Everyone complains there isn't enough good news in the papers. Now you have a remedy—the ecological programs at your camp. These make great news for local newspapers, radio, and television stations.

THE MEDIA

Before contacting the media, determine your publicity goal. Do you want to promote a new program? Or possibly highlight a new innovation? Whatever your goal, it must be newsworthy. Reporters and editors only cover subjects that are interesting to a broad base of people, not just a select group. Also, the media generally cover only one event each year that deals with your topic. Make sure that before you contact reporters and editors that you can offer the best story possible. Some newsworthy angles include: "This is the first time this has been done," "an innovative partnership with business," "a new job-skill program," "kids teach parents/grandparents," and "a family program anyone can implement."

Once you decide on your news angle, your next step is to contact the media. Look in your local newspaper for the telephone number of the "Features" or "Lifestyle" department. Call the number and ask for the editor's name and confirm the address for the newspaper.

Next, write a brief letter—no more than one page—explaining to the editor why your story is important. Suggest one or two story angles. In the last paragraph, set a time and date that you will call the editor to answer questions and to see if the paper is interested in covering the story. Then follow up!

For television stations, follow this same procedure, but ask for the name of the assignment editor at the station. In both cases, send your letter about two weeks before you want coverage.

THE EVENT

Be sure to tell people at your event that reporters might attend. When reporters do arrive, make sure you or a designated representative meet them and answer any questions they may have. Avoid suffocating the reporters; let them do their story their way, interviewing participants and shooting pictures as they need. Get signed releases from those photographed and from all campers.

After the event, watch the newspaper and television stations for coverage of your event. Be sure to clip articles and use your VCR to tape the television stories.

MORE MILEAGE

Always alert parents and board members to your camp's media coverage. You might also contact your local city and county representatives, including the mayor and your district's state and U.S. representatives, about your efforts. Be sure to display any congratulatory letters from these sources for your board and parents.

Recognition raises the camp's status in everyone's eyes. Between these letters and your news clippings, you will have some good ammunition to use when approaching parents, local businesses, and industries for donations and volunteers. When writing to your representatives in particular, it's important to ask if there is grant money available to continue and expand programs such as yours.

BEYOND THE MEDIA

CAMPERS

Your campers and staff may be the best coverage your camp and environmental programs will ever have! They are the ones who make the program happen, and they will want to know how well they did. Supply them with a review of the session's or summer's achievements, including tips on how to continue their efforts at home.

Include a basic list of books they can use to build a library, write advocacy letters, and start recycling programs at home or school. Also point them toward catalogs of ecologically sound products.

ASSOCIATIONS, MAGAZINES, AND INDUSTRIES

Let other environmentally concerned groups know about your camp's efforts. Contact industries, organizations, and associations such as those listed in Appendix A, trade groups, and affiliated interest groups. Offer to share experiences and make photos available to them.

ENVIRONMENTAL AWARENESS EDUCATION

Invite the public to your camp for an environmental education program. This gives the camp itself further exposure, opens a forum for speakers, and attracts local attention.

Program ideas include:

❏ Lectures on water conservation, pollution, or local flora and fauna;

❏ Nature hikes;

❏ Lectures or hands-on demonstrations about packaging and source reduction, recycling, and eco-wise products;

❏ Experiential education on composting and conservation products and their installation.

APPENDIX C: HOLD THAT COMPOST

WORM COMPOSTING BIN

MATERIALS LIST

1 4' x 8' sheet of $\frac{1}{2}$" outdoor plywood

1 14' outdoor 2x4

1 16' outdoor 2x4

1 lb. 4d galvanized nails

$\frac{1}{4}$ lb. 16d galvanized nails

2 3" door hinges and screws

TOOLS

tape measure

skill saw or rip hand saw

hammer

saw horses

long straight edge or chalk snap line

screwdriver

chisel

wood glue

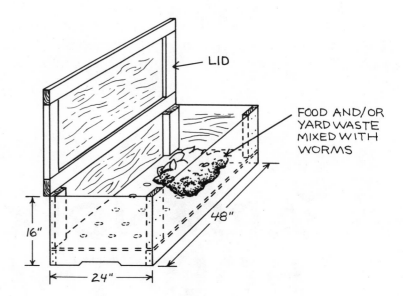

Figure C-1. Assembled worm composting bin

drill with $\frac{1}{2}''$ bit

goggles

ear protection

ASSEMBLY INSTRUCTIONS

1. Cut plywood as shown in Figure C-2.

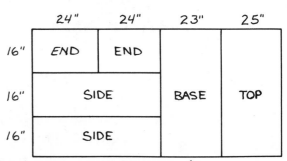

Figure C-2. 4' x 8' sheet of $\frac{1}{2}''$ plywood

2. Prepare base:
   - ❏ Cut 14' 2x4 into six pieces: one 12", two 48", and three 20" lengths.
   - ❏ Set 12" length aside until step 3 below.
   - ❏ Use 16d nails to nail together a 48" x 24" frame as shown in Figure C-3.
   - ❏ Use 4d nails to nail the base to this frame.
3. Create side panels.
   - ❏ Cut 16' 2x4 into four pieces: three 12" and one 9' length. Set aside 9' length.

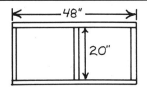

- ❏ You should now have four 12″ lengths, including the one left over from when you cut the 14′ 2x4.
- ❏ Place two 12″ lengths of 2x4 on your work surface, parallel to each other and 48″ apart.

Figure C-3. Base frame 2x4s on edge

- ❏ Set one side panel on top of 2x4s. Before nailing, line up top of 2x4 with top of panel, and side of 2x4 with side of panel. (The 2x4 should be 4″ short of the bottom edge of the panel.)
- ❏ Use 4d nails to nail plywood panel to 2x4.
- ❏ Repeat for second side panel.
- ❏ Stand side panels on end and use 4d nails to nail side panels to ends of base frame. Place a nail at least every 3″.

4. Add ends to box.
   - ❏ Use 4d nails to nail end pieces to base frame and side frame.

5. Drill twelve $\frac{1}{2}$″ holes in the bottom of the box for drainage.

6. Build and attach lid.
   - ❏ Cut the remainder of the 16′ 2x4 into four pieces: two 51″ and two 27″ lengths.
   - ❏ Cut lap joints in corners, as shown in Figure C-4, and lay out pieces as a square.
   - ❏ Use wood glue to secure frame, and then nail with 16d nails.
   - ❏ Place frame flat on working surface and lay remaining panel of plywood over frame, as shown in Figure C-5.

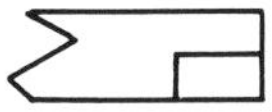

Figure C-4. End view of lap joint

   - ❏ Use 4d nails to nail plywood to 2x4 frame.
   - ❏ Use shorter screws to attach hinges to the top of the lid. Make certain screws go through both plywood and 2x4s.
   - ❏ Place lid on top of bin unit.
   - ❏ Use longer screws to attach hinges to the back of the bin.

PORTABLE WOOD AND WIRE COMPOSTING BIN

MATERIALS LIST

4 12′ outdoor 2x4s

13′ of 36″ wide $\frac{1}{2}$″ hardware cloth

36 poultry wire staples or power stapler with 1″ staples

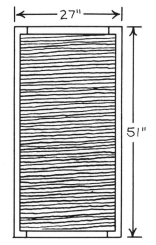

Figure C-5. Lid 2x4 frame with plywood cover

8 $\frac{1}{2}$" carriage bolts 3" long

8 washers and nuts to fit bolts

2 3" zinc-plated hinges for door

2 hook and eye screw sets (1–$\frac{1}{2}$" zinc plated or galvanized)

4 L-brackets and screws

64 1–$\frac{1}{2}$" galvanized nails

wood glue

TOOLS

hand saw or circular power saw

drill with $\frac{1}{2}$" or $\frac{1}{8}$" bit

screwdriver

hammer

tin snips

tape measure

pencil

$\frac{3}{4}$" socket or open-ended wrench

carpenter's square

goggles

ear protection

ASSEMBLY INSTRUCTIONS

1. Build four square frames from the 2x4s.
   - ❑ Cut 2x4s into twelve 3' lengths.
   - ❑ Cut 2" lap joints at each end of 3' lengths. Fit lap joints together as corners (see Figure C-7).
   - ❑ Use wood glue and nails to secure corners.

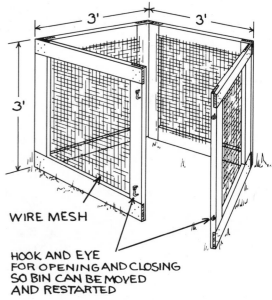

WIRE MESH

HOOK AND EYE FOR OPENING AND CLOSING SO BIN CAN BE MOVED AND RESTARTED

Figure C-6. Assembled portable composting bin

2. Cover square frames with hardware cloth.
   - ❑ Use tin snips to cut four 38" long sections of hardware cloth.
   - ❑ Bend back the top and bottom edges (1" at both ends of the 38").
   - ❑ Stretch cloth across each frame.
   - ❑ Square frame and cloth, and staple cloth to frame.
   - ❑ Bend sides of cloth around frame and staple.

3. Connect three of the four frames in a U-shape.
   ❏ Stand and arrange three frames so that from above they make a U-shape (see Figure C-8).
   ❏ Set L-brackets on corners where frames meet and mark holes for screws.
   ❏ Remove brackets and drill holes for screws.
   ❏ Replace brackets and drill holes for screws.
   ❏ Follow this procedure for both right angles.

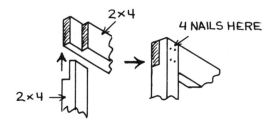

Figure C-7. End view of lap joint

4. Connect fourth frame to existing U-shape as a door.
   ❏ Stand fourth frame to complete the box.
   ❏ On the outside of one of the right angles between the door and the existing U-shape, mark the position for screws for the hinges. One hinge should be approximately 4″ from the top; the other 4″ from the bottom.
   ❏ Drill holes for screws.
   ❏ Attach hinges with screws.

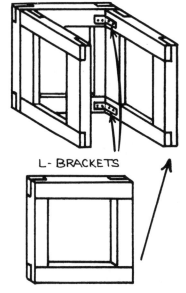

Figure C-8. Three frames in U-shape

5. Connect hook and eye sets to secure door (see Figure C-6).
   ❏ Drill holes on the door for hook. Drill one hole 4″ from top and another 4″ from bottom, on the outside edge of open side of door.
   ❏ Screw in hook.
   ❏ Close door and mark position where eye should be mounted so that hook and eye will meet.
   ❏ Drill holes and screw in eye.

INDEX